MILL'S
ON LIBERTY
A BEGINNER'S GUIDE

MILL'S
ON LIBERTY

A BEGINNER'S GUIDE

GEORGE MYERSON

Hodder & Stoughton

A MEMBER OF THE HODDER HEADLINE GROUP

For my son Simon, with love

Orders: please contact Bookpoint Ltd, 78 Milton Park, Abingdon, Oxon OX14 4TD. Telephone: (44) 01235 400400, Fax: (44) 01235 400500. Lines are open from 9.00–6.00, Monday to Saturday, with a 24-hour message answering service. Email address: orders@bookpoint.co.uk

British Library Cataloguing in Publication Data
A catalogue record for this title is available from The British Library

ISBN 0 340 80473 4

First published 2001
Impression number 10 9 8 7 6 5 4 3 2 1
Year 2007 2006 2005 2004 2003 2002

Cover photo from Corbis Images.
Typeset by Transet Limited, Coventry, England.
Printed in Great Britain for Hodder & Stoughton Educational, a division of Hodder Headline Plc, 338 Euston Road, London NW1 3BH by Cox & Wyman, Reading, Berks.

CONTENTS

FOREWORD

Welcome to …

Hodder & Stoughton's Beginner's Guides to Great Works

… your window into the world of the big ideas!

This series brings home for you the classics of western and world thought. These are the guides to the books everyone wants to have read – the greatest moments in science and philosophy, theology and psychology, politics and history. Even in the age of the Internet, these are the books that keep their lasting appeal. As so much becomes ephemeral – the text message, the e-mail, the season's hit that is forgotten in a few weeks – we have a deeper need of something more lasting. These are the books that connect the ages, shining the light of the past on the changing present, and expanding the horizons of the future.

However, the great works are not always the most immediately accessible. Though they speak to us directly, in flashes, they are also expressions of human experience and perceptions at its most complex. The purpose of these guides is to take you into the world of these books, so that they can speak directly to your experience.

WHAT COUNTS AS A GREAT WORK?

There is no fixed list of great works. Our aim is to offer as comprehensive and varied a selection as possible from among the books which include:

* **The key points of influence** on science, ethics, religious beliefs, political values, psychological understanding.

* The finest achievements of **the greatest authors**.

* The origins and climaxes in **the great movements** of thought and belief.

* The most provocative arguments, which have aroused **the strongest reactions**, including the most notorious as well as the most praised works.

* The high points of **intellectual style**, wit and persuasion.

READING THIS GUIDE

There are many ways to enjoy this book – whether you are thinking of reading the great work, or have tried and want some support, or have enjoyed it and want some help to clarify and express your reactions.

These guides will help you appreciate your chosen book if you are taking a course, or if you are following your own pathway.

What this guide offers

Each guide aims:

* To tell the whole story of the book, from its origins to its influence.

* To follow the book's argument in a careful and lively way.

* To explain the key terms and concepts.

* To bring in accessible examples.

* To provide further reading and wider questions to explore.

How to approach this guide

These guides are designed to be a coherent read, keeping you turning the pages from start to finish – maybe even in a sitting or two!

At the same time, the guide is also a reference work that you can consult repeatedly as you read the great work or after finishing a passage. To make both reading and consulting easy, the guides have:

* Key quotations with page references to different editions.

* Explanations of key quotes.

Our everyday life is buzzing with messages that get shorter and more disposable every month. Through this guide, you can enter a more lasting dialogue of ideas.

George Myerson,
Series Editor

A NOTE ABOUT QUOTATIONS

With each quotation, accompanying page references are given for three major editions:

* Penguin, *On Liberty*, edited by Gertrude Himmelfarb (Harmondsworth, 1974);
* Oxford World's Classics, *On Liberty and Utilitarianism*, edited by John Gray (Oxford, 1991);
* Norton Critical Edition *Mill*, including the complete *On Liberty*, edited by Alan Ryan (New York, 1997).

There are only minor differences of punctuation due to differing editorial judgements of readability. In the quoted passages, I have taken the most readable punctuation for our purposes, where there are these minor variations.

References are shortened to:

O: Oxford World's Classics, **P**: Penguin Classics, **N**: Norton.

MILL'S *ON LIBERTY*: SPECIAL FEATURES

This Beginner's Guide aims to bring to life the reading of this great work, and to put that reading in context. For this purpose, a number of special features are included in the text:

Key Quote Boxes: These give a touch more emphasis to the presentation of extracts that are being considered in more depth or are more central to the understanding of Mill's arguments.

Key Passage Boxes: In a few cases, longer extracts have been given the heading 'key passage' for emphasis and to highlight the different nature of their place in our discussion.

The above feature is often accompanied by a section headed ***Anatomy*** of the key quote or passage. In these anatomies, central phrases are picked out and explained in context.

Quotation Boxes: These frame passages from the original text that are woven into the guided reading.

Each of the above features is often accompanied by a section headed ***Anatomy*** of the key quote or passage. In these anatomies, central phrases are picked out and explained in context.

Explanatory Summaries: The discussion is accompanied by a number of shaded boxes that present concise summaries of Mill's main arguments, methods and values, under such individual headings as 'Mill's Reasonable Extremism', 'Liberal Vision' and 'Stages of History'. These boxes are designed to make the structure of Mill's arguments easier to follow, without breaking the flow of our reading.

Bullet points are employed to give clear summaries of the progress of our account. Chapter boxes enable you to trace the movements through Mill's text conveniently.

We hope that the result is a flowing discussion that fills in difficult points for you without too much interruption.

A GREAT WORK: JOHN STUART MILL'S *ON LIBERTY*

Published in 1859, Mill's *On Liberty* is the classic statement of the scope and limits of individual freedom. Mill's *On Liberty*:

* Brings human history to life as a 'struggle' between 'liberty' and 'authority'.
* Proposes and defends a single principle for judging the legitimacy of any interference by society in the lives of individuals. This principle remains a radical basis for arguments in our own time in defence of individuality and non-conformism.
* Gives the fullest justification for free speech and freedom of thought. Mill's arguments on liberty of the press still have a cutting edge in our own time, and provide a standard for assessing new laws in the field of 'freedom of information' and censorship.
* Makes liberty the basis for a radical theory of human well-being.

On Liberty demonstrates the value of individual freedom to the development of humanity as a whole. It remains a liberal vision for the future.

INTRODUCTION – READING *ON LIBERTY* NOW

MILL – THE MOST REASONABLE EXTREMIST
'Surely nobody can disagree ...?'

Think of your strongest moral belief: what action is most definitely right or most emphatically wrong? Think of the clearest example of a good person, or the most definitive instance of a wicked political policy. Now try to argue against yourself. What is wrong with your moral belief? What could be said against that good person? How would someone defend that political policy?

According to the Victorian philosopher of freedom, John Stuart Mill, if you cannot think of strong counter-arguments, then you do not really understand your own beliefs. Here is one of the many classic statements from his *On Liberty*, the most important defence of freedom of thought, discussion and action in the English language:

QUOTATION

He who knows only his side of the case knows little of that.

cross reference O: 42; P: 98; N: 69

If you cannot imagine what an opponent would say, a real opponent, with serious arguments and reasons, then you do not really know *why* you hold your own opinions or values. Normally, we assume that we need to know the reasons *for* our own views. Asked to explain my strongest belief, I start trotting out the positive reasons in its defence. But Mill thinks we don't truly understand the basis for our most cherished ideas and judgements – not unless we can see the objections. These strong beliefs are precisely the ones on which we have trouble imagining the other side.

Mill is uncompromising and provocative. If a person cannot come up with plausible objections to his dearest beliefs of values, then he does not really have any basis for holding them:

QUOTATION

His reasons may be good, and no one may have been able to refute them. But if he is equally unable to refute the reasons on the other side, if he does not so much as know what they are, he has no ground for preferring either opinion.

cross reference O: 42; P: 98; N: 69

Mill moves carefully from point to point. This writing is tightly reasoned. But in his own way, Mill is a natural extremist. *On Liberty* is a great work of **reasonable extremism:**

Mill's Reasonable Extremism: The Method of Arguing
Never stop short, if the argument can be taken further.

In this key passage, Mill insists that if a person does not know both sides of an issue, 'he has **no ground**' for choosing one side over the other. The 'no' is emphatic and total, typical of what makes *On Liberty* **the most provocative statement on liberal principles in the history of philosophy and political theory**. Every case has two sides, or many sides. If you only know one, then your opinions are entirely arbitrary. You are choosing your beliefs at random. Do your strongest beliefs meet this challenge? Are you sure?

How can they?

Now think of the most offensive person in the world. Everything about them is disgusting; they hold every view you despise. Their lifestyle is truly repugnant to you. Whenever he or she speaks, their views are despicable and their words degrade everything that you find valuable. You are outraged by this person's whole existence. According to Mill, your outrage is your own problem. You can try to persuade such a person to change their ways, if you can bear to talk to them. But that is all. You have no grounds for being protected from the pain of your own disgust or outrage:

> QUOTATION
>
> *There are many who consider as an injury to themselves any conduct which they have a distaste for, and resent it as an outrage to their feelings.*
>
> cross reference O: 93; P: 151; N: 106

Beyond your effort at reasoning with this objectionable person, you are not entitled to campaign against this disgusting lifestyle, or to try to get it prohibited. But Mill believes many social restrictions typify this way of thinking: people think society should protect them against the existence of lifestyles that offend them:

> QUOTATION
>
> *In its interferences with personal conduct it [the public] is seldom thinking of anything but the enormity of acting or thinking differently from itself.*
>
> cross reference O: 93; P: 151; N: 106

Mill insists that others should be absolutely free to offend us, to live the most offensive lifestyles we can imagine. This was written in 1859, when Queen Victoria was sovereign of the British Empire, but the argument still bites, as we enter the third millennium.

Whatever our dearest value, we need people to denounce and deny it! We need other people to live unacceptable lives, to make unacceptable choices. Mill's *On Liberty* is mainly an attempt to explain *why* we need the others, the dissidents and blasphemers, the misfits and nonconformists, the awkward squads of all kinds.

MILL'S LIBERAL VISION

Stay calm if there's no harm

Liberalism means many different things: a political movement, a theory, a set of values, an approach to life. There have been many liberal thinkers, and they have often disagreed – perhaps that is part of what makes them liberals! But at the centre of any liberalism is the concept of freedom. Liberal politics is the politics of freedom; liberal ethics is the ethics that starts and finishes with freedom.

Mill's *On Liberty* is one of the great liberal texts because of the argument we have begun to observe – the argument about the individual and society. Like all liberals, Mill faces a problem: surely there must be limits to this liberty? According to Mill, there is only one reason for preventing a lifestyle, or suppressing a view:

QUOTATION

...the only purpose for which power can rightfully be exercised over any member of a civilised community, against his will, is to prevent harm to others.

cross reference O: 14; P: 68; N: 48

If it isn't doing anyone any harm then it cannot legitimately be stopped. Lots of questions arise here, and we will be discussing them later. But one thing is clear: *your* sense of outrage does not count as harm. Nobody, according to this liberal vision, can claim to be harmed by views that disgust them, or lifestyles that annoy them. On the contrary, as we will see, Mill insists that offensive lives and alien views are probably necessary: they are doing you good. Society, argues this most reasonable extremist, needs blasphemers. This makes Mill's *On Liberty* one of the texts which pushes liberal thinking to the edge.

Mill's liberal vision allows only that one limit, that of 'harm to others'. There is bound to be an argument about this harm; but one thing is clear, having your feelings hurt, or your ideals besmirched, does not count as being harmed. He gives some famous examples of what does and does not count as harm:

KEY PASSAGE

Is it really doing any harm?

An opinion that corn-dealers are starvers of the poor, or that private property is robbery, ought to be unmolested when simply circulated through the press, but may justly incur punishment when delivered orally to an excited mob assembled before the house of a corn-dealer, or when handed about among the same mob in the form of a placard.

cross reference P: 119

No person ought to be punished simply for being drunk; but a soldier or a policeman should be punished for being drunk on duty.

cross reference O: 90; P: 149; N: 104

Together, these examples define Mill's liberal vision.

The first example is about freedom of expression. In 1859, most 'respectable' citizens would not have agreed that people should be free to write articles denouncing private property as theft. Mill is saying that the argument is only harmful, if you can show a direct effect of uttering those words, in that particular situation.

Mill's liberal vision: Freedom of expression
No value or institution is so important to society that it is entitled to protection from being denounced or criticised.

If someone wants to write diatribes against the family, say, or against education, or against the police, we ought to let them. In fact, we probably ought to encourage them, the more we find their views offensive. Have you no confidence in your ability to answer back?

The second example is about character and lifestyle. In our time, UK legislation is being proposed to keep those with 'personality disorders' off our streets. Mill would dissent, unless someone is actually being hurt.

Mill's liberal vision: Freedom to be yourself
People's vices, if they are vices, are none of your business, unless someone is being directly hurt.

The drunkenness example offended many Victorians – as Mill intended. This was written in the great period of the temperance movement. But just listen to contemporary British politicians talking about 'yob culture', crowds of youths on the streets! Mill insists that society has no justification for stopping anyone getting drunk, unless they are performing a public role – say an airline pilot, in contemporary discussion.

WHY READ *ON LIBERTY* NOW?

A different reason

We tend to think of reasoning as a dry process and of being 'reasonable' as mainly about calming down. Doesn't a reasonable person tend to take the middle ground, to compromise, to be, in fact, lukewarm? To read Mill's *On Liberty* is to gain a different sense of **what it means to be reasonable**. Mill's book is a work of passionate reasonableness, of reasonable extremism.

A liberal vision

The liberal argument of *On Liberty* is still very much alive in the present. These words still grab our attention, seek to persuade us that **we have not understood the basis of a free society**, that we have not gone nearly far enough in our lazy assent to the value of personal liberty. This Victorian thinker's words still accuse us of being half-hearted in our conventional acceptance of the views and lives of others. Have we really understood the implications of living in a free society, where different people truly hold diverse beliefs and live differing lifestyles? We have not yet 'caught up' with Mill's arguments.

Cultural history

In reading *On Liberty*, we are tracing **the history of our own voices** and key words. Mill's great book plays a major role in promoting a modern language of freedom. His key terms include words which are still central to our debates about liberty: 'diversity' and 'individuality', 'conformity' and 'interference'. He also helps to define major concepts like 'public opinion' and 'fashion'.

OUTLINE OF THIS GUIDE

Chapter 1 surveys Mill's life, particularly as seen in his own classic *Autobiography*, and looks briefly at his times.

Chapters 2 onwards form a guided reading of *On Liberty*. The focus is as follows:

Chapters 2 discusses the basic theory of 'liberty'. There is an explanation of the liberal heart of *On Liberty*, and of the relationship between Mill's liberalism and his wider philosophy of 'utility' (*On Liberty*, 'Introductory').

Chapter 3 explains the other side of Mill's basic position, his account of history as the struggle between liberty and authority. Though Mill is most well known for his hard-edged principles of freedom, he himself always relates theory to actual history. Indeed Mill's idea of history is integral to his theory of freedom (*On Liberty*, 'Introductory').

Chapters 4 and 5 explain the main arguments that Mill offers on 'Freedom of Discussion and Thought'. First we look at his classic dissection of conventional ideas about liberty of the press. A contemporary example is employed: The UK Freedom of Information Act. Second, we examine how Mill systematically destroys conventional assumptions about the limits of free expression (*On Liberty*, II).

Chapter 6 introduces Mill's radical defence of 'individuality' and his wider theory of human well-being. The account is presented in terms of key sayings or proverbs of well-being, vivid formulations that light up Mill's argument (*On Liberty*, III).

Chapter 7 considers Mill's vision of his own society, and how far that social criticism is still applicable to our day (*On Liberty*, end of III, 'Of Individuality', IV 'The Individual and Society' and V 'Applications').

Mill's life story

In his *Autobiography*, John Stuart Mill wrote a classic life story, one which has provided a model for many later accounts of personal crisis and recovery. The eminent philosopher, Isaiah Berlin, has called this book '*one of the most moving accounts of a human life*'. In this chapter, we follow Mill's life story, putting the tale in context. This story is related directly to the key concepts of *On Liberty*. At the heart of both works, there is a deep commitment to individuality as the source of human well-being. This story is more than just an external background for *On Liberty*; it is part of the same world.

THE EARLY YEARS

John Stuart Mill was born on 20 May 1806 in London. His father was the influential radical thinker James Mill. In his *Autobiography*, Mill gives one of the most famous accounts of a childhood, certainly of a philosopher's childhood. Interpretations have differed radically but everyone, including Mill, agrees that he had an extraordinary childhood, and that it shaped his later life as a thinker. Essentially, Mill tells us how his father educated him at home from an extremely early age until he went off to work in his father's office at the age of 18. John Stuart Mill did not go to school or university. Instead his father established for him a unique experiment in education. At age three, Mill was learning ancient Greek and arithmetic. Soon he was being taken by his father on walks across the fields and reciting the evidence of his day's reading:

> *I made notes on slips of paper while reading, and from these, in the morning walks, I told the story to him; for the books were chiefly histories, of which I read a great number: Robertson' histories, Hume, Gibbon.*

Soon Mill was reading Millar's *Historical View of the English Government* … Mosheim's *Ecclesiastical History*, McCrie's *Life of John Knox.*'

At the age of eight, Mill began Latin, and this part of his life story is a long list of books in different languages. Several of these childhood texts are directly relevant to *On Liberty*, particularly ancient works of political theory by Plato, Aristotle and Cicero. From the age of 12, Mill was taught logic, on which, in adult life , he became a leading authority. He was also kept busy reading the proofs of his father's own massive *History of British India*, which came out in 1818. Mill looked back on this work with admiration:

> **Saturated as the book is with the opinions and modes of judgement of a democratic radicalism then regarded as extreme.**

Mill also draws our attention to missing elements in this education, notably the absence of religion, for which he remains grateful. On the other hand, he does look back on a more damaging absence, the lack of affection. For some readers, notably Mill's friend Carlyle, this is the account of a nightmare childhood. For others, such as the contemporary philosopher Jonathan Riley, the verdict is more mixed, as it seems to have been for Mill himself. Many of his father's political ideas continue to find expression within *On Liberty*, but in other ways, as Isaiah Berlin observes, the book can be seen as a reaction against such an upbringing – given its emphasis upon the well-being of the individual and upon the need for people to find their own way of living and thinking.

PERSONAL CRISIS

Mill's father found a post in the East India Company, which was then responsible for the administration of India. In 1823 he found employment for his son, who remained there for 35 years, rising to a high level, until the responsibility for India passed to the Crown.

In the early 1820s Mill began a phase of active involvement in the radical political and intellectual circles of the time. In the winter of 1822–3 he set up a debating society dedicated to the ideas of utilitarianism, the philosophy espoused by his father and by the leading figure, Jeremy Bentham, who was a friend of the Mill family. We will be considering 'utility' as a key element of the arguments of *On Liberty*. The classic account of 'utility' was provided by Bentham himself:

> *An action then may be said to be comfortable to the principle of utility … when the tendency it has to augment the happiness of the community is greater than any it has to diminish it.*
>
> An Introduction to the Principles of Morals and Legislation

The famous shorthand for 'utility' was 'the greatest happiness of the greatest number', a phrase originally used by the eighteenth-century radical Joseph Priestley and taken over by Bentham. These were the ideas that lay behind the development of utilitarianism, which was the philosophy with which Mill remained engaged throughout his life, though in an increasingly subtle and critical way. In 1823, Mill was involved in the start-up of the radical journal *The Westminster Review*. In 1824-5, he was busy editing Bentham's papers on law. Between 1825 and 1830 Mill was a leading speaker on behalf of the ideas of The Utilitarian Society.

However, at the same time, Mill touchingly records that he experienced a period of deep personal crisis from 1826. It is the honest and authentic account of this personal crisis that has made his *Autobiography* a classic of literature and not merely a background to the philosophy. This is a startlingly modern story of a psychological breakdown and the long road to recovery.

The crisis story is also directly relevant in several different ways to the understanding of *On Liberty*. Mill starts by saying that in the autumn of 1826, he '*was in a dull state of nerves.*' Soon, he was overtaken by the experience of emptiness, his own life seemed without purpose or value. In this '*dry heavy dejection*', he felt alone. In particular, he knew he could never approach his dominating father with such feelings. The recovery was also an intellectual revolution. In this story, Mill tells us of his growing recognition of '*the necessities of human well-being.*' We shall see that well-being is a central subject in *On Liberty*, and the topic on which Mill continued to speak to the future in important ways. Above all, influenced especially by the poetry of Wordsworth, Mill grasped for the first time, the value of 'the internal culture of the individual'.

From 1829, Mill did not attend the debating society. He declared that he left behind the old '*system of political philosophy*' and replaced it with '*a conviction that the true system was something much more complex and many-sided*'. It is this ideal that found expression in *On Liberty* – where many-sidedness is both the content and the approach taken. His ideas were now open to a wider range of influences, including Carlyle, personally and as a writer, and Coleridge, as well as German philosophy. Mill remained a radical and a supporter of the 1830 French Revolution, but he no longer shared what now seemed his father's uncritical support for democracy as the answer to everything.

In 1830 Mill met Harriet Taylor, the love of his life. She was married with children but Harriet became his close friend and, after her husband's death in 1849, they married, in 1851. Her death from tuberculosis occurred shortly before the completion and publication of the great book *On Liberty*, which was dedicated to her memory. Indeed Mill credits Harriet with effectively being the joint author of this and a number of other works

WRITINGS

John Stuart Mill was an immensely prolific writer, contributing a huge number of articles to different journals. He also wrote a number of works which had an immediate influence at the time, and continue to be important today:

Influential works

o **In the spring of 1843, he published the great *System of Logic,* defending the view '*which derives all knowledge from experience*'. This remains a major text in the development of modern logic.**

o **In 1848, he published *Principles of Political Economy,* an immediately influential radical view of the economy.**

o **In 1854, he wrote a short version of the idea that became *On Liberty.* In 1855 he began to turn it into a book.**

In the *Autobiography,* he puts stress on this project being a joint work with Harriet. In his view, '*The Liberty is likely to survive longer than anything else that I have written.*' He sees it as '*a kind of philosophic text-book of a single truth*' and a declaration of '*the importance, to man and society, of a large variety in types of character, and of giving full freedom to human nature to expand itself in innumerable and conflicting directions.*'

There was also a dark side to Mill's view of the value of *On Liberty.* In the future, he believed, society may become more oppressive of the individual and '*It is then that the teachings of the* Liberty *will have their greatest value.*'

This is a philosophy for the future. It was also a book which had an immediate impact when it appeared in 1859, the year Darwin's *Origin of Species* was also published. Though contemporaries were hostile to many of Mill's arguments, notably his critique of their own time, the sheer attention paid to it initiated a phase when Mill became almost a dominating influence. In 1865 he became an MP, campaigning for women's suffrage, and his writings continued, including the great *Autobiography,* which was published in the year of his death, 1873.

2 Liberty in theory

This is the first of two chapters explaining the basics of Mill's arguments as he presents them in the classic 'Introductory' section of *On Liberty*. Mill uses this opening in two ways. First, he sets out his vision in 'Theory' and second, he puts his whole argument in historical perspective. In this chapter, we will examine the theoretical basis of *On Liberty*; the next chapter looks at Mill's view of the history of liberty.

PROLOGUE TO A THEORY: DEFINING 'LIBERTY'
Mill starts by defining the 'liberty' with which he is concerned:

> KEY QUOTE
> *Civil or Social liberty: the nature and limits of the power which can legitimately be exercised by society over the individual.*
> cross reference O: 5; P: 59; N: 41

Anatomy of the Key Quote

o '*Civil or Social*': Mill is not concerned with human free will under God, say, or freedom and fate. His 'liberty' is part of the way human beings exist together, as groups, as societies. It is also worth noting that he does not refer to 'political' liberty, for reasons we will soon see.

o '*power*': Mill typically thinks in negatives. So he approaches 'liberty' by bringing in 'power'. Liberty is defined as the limitation placed upon the exercise of power.

o '*legitimately*': From the start, this argument is about value judgements. Mill wants to make us think about society as a whole. For him, liberty defines a **legitimate society**. If a society exercises power in ways that overstep the bounds set by liberty, then that society fails Mill's **Liberal Legitimacy Test** which we will be discussing later. This is probably the most influential outcome of Mill's argument.

o '*society*' and *'the individual'*: This is another antithesis, like liberty and power. The sphere of individuality is defined by the limits of social intervention.

In this key quote, we see Mill thinking in opposites. He understands the meaning of each of the concepts in terms of its opposite but Mill has a particular approach to these oppositions, these binary poles. He approaches them dynamically. He does not establish fixed definitions: this is what society means, that is what the individual means. Instead, Mill is interested in the changing impacts of each concept on the other. If we look at society in this way, then what effect does that have on our view of the individual? In other words, his approach is **dialectical**. He thinks in moving oppositions.

In following through from this key passage, Mill declares that this problem of **liberty** is '*a question seldom stated*'. His aim, he implies, is precisely to state, with new clarity, the liberty question.

Mill's aims

✳ Mill aims to express the question of liberty in a new way. His view is that this 'question' has not even received proper discussion.

✳ Language is important to Mill. He wants to make it possible to state what has previously been unstated.

✳ His widest aim is to achieve an advance in the language of political and moral debate.

This unstated question, liberty, is, according to Mill, latent in many other disputes. Here we have a definition of the task of philosophy:

to state clearly the question which lies behind public conflict and debate or controversies. It seems possible that the larger aim is to make new agreement possible.

The philosopher reveals the question that is the source of disturbances in the society. All kinds of issues are difficult to resolve, until this underlying question becomes clear.

MILL'S LIBERAL LEGITIMACY TEST

Mill is not concerned to state the question of liberty purely as an intellectual exercise. In restating liberty, he is also proposing a new standard to be applied in debates about the individual and society.

Liberalism is often assumed to have a wishy-washy outlook, appealing in its openness but also unable to take a clear line. Liberals are seen as easy relativists, settling for splitting the difference between differing views. It is true that Mill often argues from the principle that the human viewpoint is inherently limited, that we live our lives in perspectives that aren't absolute, and that what you see depends on who and where you are. We see the world according to our point of view. Mill is not a relativist when it comes to evaluating a society. Here he thinks he has come up with a **standard test of the legitimacy of any society**, a test provided by his doctrine of liberty.

We have seen Mill defining liberty as the concept that fixes the legitimate uses of power in and by a society. From this follows, as we will see, a wider approach to judging both policies and societies as a whole:

Mill's Liberal Legitimacy Test
Any society that fails to honour the liberty of the individual is illegitimate. Its use of power cannot be justified if it trespasses on the rightful sphere of individuality.

This legitimacy test is liberal in that it starts from the question of freedom. An alternative legitimacy test, for example, might be based on a criterion of equality – that a legitimate society must achieve as much equality as possible.

Now we need to look at the way Mill develops his idea of liberty into this basis for social judgement. Having defined the term liberty in opposition to power, Mill then offers his principle for testing any given use of authority, any intervention by society into the life of the individual:

KEY QUOTE

The object of this Essay is to assert one very simple principle, as entitled to govern absolutely the dealings of society with the individual in the way of compulsion and control.

cross reference O: 14; P: 68; N: 48

Anatomy of the Key Quote

o *'principle'*: First, the object of the essay is to assert a **principle**. This raises the issue of what counts as a principle in general. When is an idea or argument also a principle? That turns out to be a very difficult and central question in the interpretation of Mill, and also then, in, the history of political theory.

For Mill, a principle is a proposition that supplies us with the key to a way of thinking about particular issues. To be a principle, this proposition must apply across the board. On the other hand, a principle is not an automatic solution to any specific issue. Principles need to be applied. They are not the same as rules, as John Gray shows in his influential rereading of *On Liberty*. What makes Mill's essay radical is that he claims to have discovered the principle for deciding when a society is exercising its power legitimately and when, by contrast, it has overstepped the mark. This is an absolutely huge claim. Principles are rare. There are never going to be many coherent principles. In fact, Mill might well argue that our society at present lacks any clear sense of fundamental principles altogether.

o *'one very simple principle'*: Principles are ways of thinking consistently. The aim is to show how we need only 'one principle' as the basis for our thinking about many different issues.

o *'compulsion and control'*: This principle applies both to legal penalties and to the moral coercion of public opinion. Early critics, like James Stephen, objected violently to this constraint on moral pressure: these were, after all, Victorian times! In other words, Mill is interested in the law, but he is also concerned with the general climate. He wants to know where the law should intervene on, say, drug-taking or fox-hunting. But he also wants to specify the point beyond which society should cease to exert moral pressure in more general ways.

Mill wants us to be consistent across politics and civil society. He will not accept the idea of substituting intense moral pressure for legal sanctions. They are not identical, and we can look at them differently. The case for legal sanctions must be more difficult to make and defend in the end, but still, Mill isn't going to allow a society to replace draconian laws with moral blackmail.

Mill then moves on to the most famous formulation in the book:

KEY QUOTE

That principle is, that the sole end for which mankind are warranted, individually or collectively, in interfering with the liberty of action of any of their number is self-protection ... the only purpose for which power can be rightfully exercised over any member of a civilised community, against his will, is to prevent harm to others.

cross reference O: 14; P: 68; N: 48

Anatomy of the Key Quote

- *'self-protection'*: There is a positive version of the principle of self-protection, which actually comes before the more famous negative version: *'to prevent harm to others'*. To make sense of this pairing, you have to see the 'self' in self-protection as referring to society as a whole, rather than individuals. This is not a theory of justified self-defence; it is about the extent to which a society can limit the action of individuals.

- *'mankind'*: A principle is universal, if it is truly a principle. This is what makes Mill's argument both exciting and alien. We are not used to such criteria. We have all sorts of beliefs, which we think of as generally valid: people should not be cruel, say, or kindness is better than intimidation; but we don't quite make the leap that Mill demands of his argument here. He is insisting that this principle applies to mankind as a whole, across all of time and space, throughout history.

- *'civilised community'*: There is one implied exception: *'any member of a civilised community.'* The principle is universal but there are places where it does not make sense to apply it, and that is where a society is, in Mill's terms, not (yet) civilized. In an uncivilized state, Mill concedes, it will be necessary at times to limit individual action more rigorously than in a civilized state. When you think about the context, you can see that this turns out be a controversial assumption. This book was written at the height of the British Empire, by a man with a career in Indian administration. Mill was certainly a 'progressive' in his attitude to the empire but his argument still implies a rigid distinction between people who count as civilized and others. This approach has struck some later commentators, notably Gray, as too rigid for our times.

Any society that uses power differently violates legitimate limits. At the centre of Mill's theory of liberty is his ' Harm Criterion'. If you cannot show that an act will harm someone, then you are not entitled to prevent that act – either by law or by social pressure.

> Liberal Legitimacy Test: The Harm Criterion
> *There is only one ground for restricting individuals, and that is when what they are doing will harm other people. A society is legitimate if it exercises power within those limits. Any other exercise of power is illegitimate.*

A society violates human liberty if acts are prevented beyond the Harm Criterion. This is a big idea and certain questions arise immediately. As critics from Hutton in 1859 onwards have wondered, what exactly counts as harm? Clearly physical injury is harmful but you can't say a society is entitled only to regulate its members by preventing them physically attacking one another! Fraud, forgery, and robbery of all kinds, deception, some lies: a long list of other kinds of harm unfolds immediately. Then there is the more difficult area. What about emotional and psychological damage? Is hurting someone's feelings doing him or her harm? And who gets to decide if someone's feelings are legitimately hurt by an act, or by an utterance?

How far is this principle meant to go? It seems to tell us how to set certain limits but you wouldn't be able to use this principle to decide what was a good law, say; only to decide what was a legitimate law, and what was a law too far.

Mill's Liberal Legitimacy Test: An example

Drugs and hunting are two issues on which there is widespread debate and division. They are the issues of our time. In each case, the question can be put in Mill's terms: What is the extent of '*the power which can legitimately be exercised by society over the individual*'. In the case of drugs, the problem is how far society has a duty to protect individuals from themselves. In the case of hunting, the issue is how far the disapproval of one section of society can or should be legally enforced over another.

Mill does not offer a simple way to resolve such disputes but his theory provides a way of getting the issues clear. Let's take two people:

Jake, an 18-year-old student, is strongly in favour of a ban on fox-hunting. He believes that this activity violates animal rights and he wants this outrage expressed in law. He also thinks that soft drugs should be legalized, that it is a violation of the rights of the individual to be told that he cannot explore the experience of say Ecstasy, or cannabis. Why should whisky be legal, when dope isn't?

Margaret, a 43-year-old mother and rural shopkeeper, is strongly opposed to the fox-hunting ban. She thinks it is outrageous interference by strangers in the life of her community. She is also strongly against the legalization of drugs and thinks that there needs to be a strong campaign to enforce the law on such matters.

Mill does not want us to leap to one side or the other on such issues. He wants us:

* First, to identify the underlying question: liberty, the extent of the legitimate power of society over individuals.

* Second, to apply 'one …principle' to all such 'controversies'.

For both Jake and Margaret, the two controversies, fox-hunting and drug legalization, are entirely separate matters. This is what Mill denies and, in doing so, he challenges the entire nature of all our opinions and judgements. From Mill's point of view, our judgements are *unprincipled*. We have beliefs and opinions, but we never subject these beliefs to the *test of principle*. Are we thinking consistently? Do the opinions that we have about, say, hunting bans fit with our views about drug legalization? I think the answer is often that we are effectively unprincipled in our beliefs. It is not just individuals who are unprincipled either – politics is, in this sense, unprincipled. We often hear about politicians lacking principles in a different sense. What this usually means is that they are not scrupulous enough about taking favours. But Mill's essay suggests that our whole political sphere is devoid of principle. Political parties take up positions on individual issues without any clear sense of whether those positions have a consistent basis.

BEYOND LIBERTY?

In setting out the basics of his theory, Mill immediately faces a wider problem. How many other principles are we going to need? And how are those other principles going to relate to this 'one simple principle' of liberty and its use in practice to determine the legitimacy of the uses of power. In two important ways, Mill does look 'beyond liberty'.

The Rationality Criterion

First, there is a criterion that limits the whole application of liberty. We have already touched on this, but Mill now faces it squarely:

KEY QUOTE

Liberty, as a principle, has no application to any state of things anterior to the time when mankind have become capable of being improved by free and equal discussion.

cross reference O: 15; P: 69; N: 49

Anatomy of the Key Quote

- '*capable*': In effect, Mill has defined civilization here. A civilized state is one where people have become capable of certain relationships to one another and to their society.

○ '*improved*': This is a dangerous term for Mill to have invoked.
   We will see him objecting to the desire to improve others. But
   here he means that civilized people will improve without
   compulsion – freely.

○ '*free and equal discussion*': In a civilized state, individuals have
   become capable of responding to the reasoning of others. This
   is a strong idea, and it goes way beyond liberty itself.

Alongside his famous Harm Criterion, then, Mill adds this
Rationality Criterion. In Mill's argument, this Rationality Criterion
comes before the Liberal Legitimacy Test. You have to show that a
society meets the Rationality Criterion before you are entitled to
apply a liberty test at all. In a pre-civilized society, all kinds of
interference with the individual may be legitimate. This means that
liberty cannot be Mill's sole value, or even his main value. He must
have other axes to grind.

The ultimate appeal: utility
Mill is one of the founding thinkers of modern liberalism, and his
liberty principle belongs in the tradition of liberal thought.
However, as we saw in the last chapter, he also belongs to the
philosophical school known as 'Utilitarianism', one of the most
influential approaches of nineteenth and twentieth-century
philosophy. At the same time as he wrote *On Liberty*, Mill also wrote
his definitive work on this 'Utilitarianism', defining the basis of that
wider approach to life.

We have seen that the key concept in utilitarian thought is not
liberty, but utility. Critics have accused Mill of failing to deal
coherently with the relationship of utility to liberty. By utility is
meant the happiness-producing or pain-reducing power of any act
or decision or state of affairs. According to utilitarian thought, we
must refer to such utility in making our choices. We should choose
the option that has the great utility, which means producing the

most pleasure or the least pain. This does not mean just for me; it means for everyone affected – so it is not simply a selfish approach. Mill immediately connects this view of utility to his argument about liberty:

KEY QUOTE

I regard utility as the ultimate appeal on all ethical questions; but it must be utility grounded on the permanent interests of man as a progressive being.

cross reference O: 15; P: 70; N: 49

Anatomy of the Key Quote

- '*ultimate*': When it comes to practical decision-making, what takes precedence is utility. You choose on the basis of the happiness-inducing, or pain-reducing, effects of your choice.

- '*permanent interests*': Both words are critical. Mill is not talking about transient effects, the passing pleasure of one person; he is concerned with lasting consequences, benefits and costs that do not fade with their context. This question of how interests are defined has been much discussed, notably by Berlin.

- '*man as a progressive being*': Authentic utility is what would make a rational person happy – or what would contribute to the growing happiness of the human race as a maturing entity though history.

We now have the outlines of Mill's approach – and the most important point is that he has several ideas, not one. Though this book is about one major question, the individual and society, Mill is definitely not the kind of thinker who believes he can stick to one single idea.

At the centre of the argument about liberty is the Liberal Legitimacy Test with the Harm Criterion: no harm equals no restriction.

But in two key ways Mill also needs to look beyond liberty:

1 The Rationality Criterion: no civilized reasoning means no question of liberty.

2 The ultimate appeal – utility: always choose in the interests of human happiness in the largest sense.

Mill's real problem is how these ideas relate to each other. This is not just a personal problem, it is the key difficulty which liberal theory has to overcome. Individual liberty is necessary, but not sufficient to define a good society, or a right policy or use of power.

For some critics, Mill does not give a definite enough answer to the problem of reconciling liberty with rationality and utility. He is sometimes seen as being a utilitarian in liberal clothing – smuggling a utility dogma in under the pretence of defending individual freedom. Others accuse him of shuffling from one concept to another when it suits his argument.

Two points may be made in Mill's defence:

1 Mill is a dialectical thinker. He does not offer a rule or a system, he proposes concepts that we have to balance against each other. This process of balancing is dialectical, in the sense that we are weighing different forces, pulling in contrary directions. Mill aims to start a process, not give a solution.

2 The liberty principle is *not* Mill's 'ultimate' test for specific choices or policies. This is important, because it distinguishes Mill from many other thinkers and a great deal of modern politicians. No one has been more serious about freedom than Mill – but he does not have the illusion that the first person to refer to freedom in an argument will be on the winning side. Yet that is pretty much how a lot of modern political and cultural debate has worked.

3 Liberty in history

We have seen how Mill proposes a theory of freedom and how that theory has been hugely influential. But in fact, there is another side to Mill's view of freedom – an historical dimension. In this chapter, we explore Mill's version of human history as the evolution of liberty. Without this history, the theory hangs in a vacuum. Mill is not really the kind of thinker who works in abstract formulae. He seeks always to connect his principles with actual societies and real histories, as he understands them. In fact, *On Liberty* is at least as much a vision of history as it is an argument about values.

THE PROGRESSIVE BEING OF HUMANITY

In the previous chapter, we saw how Mill defined his principle of utility as referring to the lasting benefit of '*man as a progressive being*'. History is the field where this 'progressive being' finds expression but there is nothing complacent or simple about Mill's version of historical progress.

For Mill, as for Marx, history does not mean the past or past events. Both thinkers see the present as a phase in a process that connects all that has been with the possible future. In other words, history is a living process, which includes his own age:

KEY QUOTE

...the stage of progress into which the more civilised portions of the species have now entered.

cross reference O: 5; P: 59; N: 41

Anatomy of the Key Quote

o *'stage'*: We tend to talk in terms of historical 'periods', neutral and directionless slices of time. By comparison, for Mill, a 'stage' suggests an unfolding trajectory. This is an approach also found in Marx, in Hegel and in Comte. There is an analogy implied between historical progress and individual growth. It is as if there was a natural progression from less advanced stage to more advanced.

o *'civilised portions'*: Mill's arguments involve a strong sense of the one-ness of humanity. Though some parts are, in his terms, more civilized, they still belong to the whole. We have seen that civilized for Mill, refers not to moral or technological development, but to 'free and equal discussion'.

o *'species'*: As we saw, Mill's *On Liberty* was published in 1859, the same year as Darwin's *Origin of Species*. Behind the logic of human history, there is the pattern of natural history.

It always seems to us that Victorian ideas of progress are complacent. Why should one assume that history was naturally moving forwards? The crises of the twentieth century seem to have undermined this assumption of a trajectory through time, but there is, in fact, another way of holding a belief in progress. Far from being complacent about the present, Mill uses the idea of progress to challenge his own time. The present itself is simply a stage. There will be a future from whose point of view this moment will be as limited as the dark ages now seem to the Victorians era.

The first feature of history is progress – but the second feature is struggle:

KEY QUOTE

The struggle between Liberty and Authority is the most conspicuous feature in the portions of history with which we are earliest familiar.

cross reference O: 5; P: 59; N: 41

Anatomy of the Key Quote

o *'earliest'*: Where does history start? What is the first scene of the drama? For Mill, history begins as 'struggle'. No doubt, there are phases before struggle, but they do not merit the title of history at all. What counts as historical time is defined by conflict. History is the story of a fundamental antithesis, and society comes into existence as the medium through which certain oppositions fight for supremacy.

o *'struggle'*: This idea of history as 'struggle' is central to the philosophy of Hegel, the dominant influence on nineteenth-century philosophy of history. In his thought, oppositions drive history forwards between ideas.

1 Marx takes over Hegel's approach to history as 'struggle.' In the 1848 *Communist Manifesto*, history is a series of stages in the class struggle.

2 The term for this view of history is 'dialectical'.

In Hegel, the dialectic was a struggle between ideas. In Marx, dialectic was the conflict between social forces, called classes. The nineteenth century was the phase of the conflict between the bourgeois class and the working class. Mill has his own version of the dialectic, as the unfolding of the conflict between freedom and its antitheses at different stages of human and social development.

THE DIALECTIC OF LIBERTY

In the previous chapter, we saw how Mill defined a liberty principle in universal terms: liberty is the criterion by which we decide on the legitimate relations between society and the individual. But now we see his other perspective. Liberty has a history, in which it means different things as it encounters changing counterforces.

Milll's Dialectic of Liberty
Human history expresses the struggle between two principles: liberty and authority.

Mill surveys history, as 'we' know it: Greece, Rome and England. There is, as Gray emphasizes, something surprisingly unquestioning about Mill's assumptions that history belongs in the West, and that it begins in classical Greece particularly. There is also something oddly naïve about the way he attaches England to classical Greece and Rome. This is more Victorian mythology than history in a modern sense. On the other hand, within that limitation, Mill has an interesting view of the shape of history.

The first stage: the tyrannical era

In the first stage, liberty comes into being as the opposite of **tyranny**:

QUOTATION
By liberty, was meant protection against the tyranny of the political rulers.

cross reference **O: 5; P: 59; N: 41**

Mill's history starts as total oppression:

Mill's Dialectic of Liberty
First stage: The Era of Original Tyranny
In the time of the tyrants, Liberty is the people's shield against absolute rule.

During the first stage the rulers believe they can do as they please; they think of their subjects as mere objects to be used at will. Mill defines this original society as 'political tyranny'. Politics begins as tyranny, not as freedom. Liberty is born as the enemy of this version of politics.

> Definition: 'political'
> *'The political' starts as pure power; liberty begins as the alternative to 'political power'.*

In the first stage of history, the tyrannical era, politics is born to express the will of the rulers. Everything else is outside the political sphere. This is important because it means that liberty does not begin as a political principle, but rather as the opposite of 'the political'. Liberty is the counter-value to the will of the rulers:

QUOTATION

The rulers were conceived … as a necessarily antagonistic position to the people whom they ruled.

cross reference O: 5; P: 59; N: 41

Greek democracy is seen as an early exception – a sign of things to come. But in the main, the first phase has a clear meaning: rulers against ruled.

In the first phase, liberty emerges as the **principle of society**, to set against the rule of politics. The rulers begin politics; liberty is begun by the ruled. Therefore, Mill does not see liberty as a political principle but rather as a social principle, defined in opposition to the realm of political power. The state is not the natural source of liberty, but rather its original enemy. Liberty is born outside politics.

> Definition: Original liberty
> *Liberty is created by society in the face of political power.*

Liberty is the concept that the ruled develop to resist political tyranny. In dialectical terms, it is tyranny that gives birth to liberty.

The whole of Mill's approach is implicit in this starting-point. This original concept of liberty is a negative idea, a reaction against tyranny. Famously, Rousseau declared that man was born free: that can be called romantic liberty. For Mill, as for Marx, liberty is born out of social resistance to oppression. Freedom is not the original state of individuals. On the contrary, freedom is born in the struggle of society to resist the absolute will of the original tyrants. This is important because Mill is traditionally criticized for being too much of an individualist. Here we can see that, in fact, Mill conceives of liberty itself as a *social* creation.

The second stage: the birth of democracy

Each stage of history is defined by its own concept of liberty. In the first phase, liberty means the 'limitation' of the absolute power of the political rulers. The second stage begins when the people begin to enter the political sphere. Now liberty loses its previous meaning. In the second stage, a new struggle begins:

QUOTATION

As the struggle proceeded for making the ruling power emanate from the periodical choice of the ruled.

cross reference O: 7; P: 61; N: 42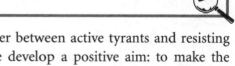

Now the struggle is no longer between active tyrants and resisting subjects. Instead, the people develop a positive aim: to make the rulers into vehicles of their will. This second phase is the birth of democratic society and its key event is the French Revolution.

Mill's Dialectic of Liberty
Second stage: The Birth of Democracy
The democratic spirit seeks to seize power for society. Liberty is
no longer the shield of the ruled against the rulers, but part of
the demand for power.

Since the people aim to take power, they do not need an idea of
liberty as the defence against that power. Instead, they assume that
once they have power, they will necessarily be free.

> KEY QUOTE
> *The nation did not need to be protected against its own*
> *will.*
>
> cross reference O: 7; P: 61; N: 43

Anatomy of the Key Quote

o '*nation*': This is the central concept of nineteenth-century
   politics and history. The birth of democracy is part of the self-
   expression of the nation, what is still called 'national self-
   determination'.

o '*will*': There are many versions of the idea of the 'will' in
   nineteenth-century philosophy. Rousseau based his theory of
   democracy on an idea of 'the general will' of the people.

Second stage: liberty
Liberty means access to power, not protection against power.

When the people are in power, tyranny is surely impossible. If the
nation itself is the ruler: '*There was no fear of its tyrannizing over*
itself.'

In the first phase, there was a conflict between rulers and ruled, between politics and society. In the second stage, the ruled aspire to become the rulers and society takes command of politics for itself. Politics is reborn as the process by which society governs itself. In that context, it appears as if the old idea of liberty is redundant.

This is a good example of Mill's dialectical view of liberty. As society goes through different phases, the meaning of liberty actually changes. There are two sides to this history of liberty. On the one hand, an idea does seem to march through history – the idea of freedom. On the other hand, that idea is interpreted in radically new ways by each new era.

The third stage: the tyranny of the majority
A third phase is already implied. In this next phase, the rule of the people gives birth to a new kind of tyranny – '*the tyranny of the majority*' (cross reference **O**: 8, **P**: 63, **N**: 44).

In the third stage of this dialectic of liberty, the rule of the people becomes a new tyranny. In fact, of course, there was far from a pure democracy in Mill's time – he himself campaigned for a widening of the vote, particularly to include women – but by the tyranny of the majority he meant something more than a merely electoral effect:

KEY QUOTE

…when society is itself the tyrant – society collectively over the separate individuals who compose it – its means of tyrannizing are not restricted to the acts which it may do by the hands of its political functionaries.

cross reference O: 8; P: 63; N: 44

Anatomy of the Key Quote

- '*collectively*': This is an early example of the negative use of 'collective' in opposition to 'individuals'. In this key passage, we see a paradox of social being. Society is made of individuals; yet the collective takes on its own life, and turns itself into the enemy of each and every 'separate' individual.

- '*political functionaries*': This is a satirical term for the elected leaders and representatives in a democratic system. The word 'funtionaries' implies a bureaucratic role. When Mill stood as an MP, he warned the electors that he would not be bound by their wishes!

The majority has many ways of imposing its will. Politics is merely one weapon of the majority in its effort to force all minorities to conform. In the third phase, the struggle is between a tyrannical majority and oppressed minorities.

Mill's Dialectic Of Liberty	Social structure	Power structure
Phase one	Original society	Absolute rulers against the people
Phase two	The democratic upheaval	The people take control of their rulers
Phase three	Settled democracy	The tyranny of the majority

The struggle began as a battle between rulers and ruled, tyrants and people. In between there is the birth of **democracy**. Now the struggle is between a dominant majority and excluded minorities, or even every individual as a distinct being. To start with, society was under the thumb of power politics, but now society itself has become the oppressor: '*society collectively*'. This third phase is the struggle between the collective spirit and the individual, between conformity and difference. The third phase is the era of **social oppression**.

It is clear that Mill thinks his own society has entered this third phase, though it still has some way to go. In effect, this is the era of modern society, or mass society. What does liberty mean now? Liberty must be reborn as the counter-principle not to the absolute rulers, but to the majority:

> QUOTATION
> *There is a limit to the legitimate interference of collective opinion with individual independence.*
>
> cross reference O: 9; P: 63; N: 44

> Mill's Dialectic of Liberty
> *Third stage: Settled Democracy*
> *Liberty means the limitation on the tyranny of the majority over minorities, and individuals.*

Across history, the meaning of liberty has reversed: this is the dialectic of the idea. To start with, liberty meant the protection of the vast majority against the arbitrary will of the rulers. By this third stage, liberty means the protection of others against the arbitrary will of the majority. The meaning of liberty changes as the nature of tyranny alters. In effect, each new phase of tyranny gives birth to its own corresponding idea of liberty. This is the essence of Mill's dialectical view of history.

Mill's own theory of liberty belongs to the third phase, 'the tyranny of the majority'. He has a very dark view indeed of this phase. In previous eras, tyranny was external: brute force, physical violence. It was also possible to fight back through action. But now the tyranny has become internal: it hides and grows inside each person. 'Social tyranny' is worse than 'political oppression', for Mill, because it is so much harder to overcome:

> QUOTATION
>
> *...it leaves fewer means of escape, penetrating much more deeply into the details of life, and ensalving the soul itself.*
>
> cross reference O: 9; P: 63; N: 44

This is the darkest moment in *On Liberty*, a moment of bitter pessimism. This side of the book is often overlooked, the emphasis falling upon the positive philosophy of freedom, and on the formula for applying it to – the Harm Criterion. But Mill also has this dark side to his outlook. He sees progress itself as giving rise to a new and more frightening kind of oppression.

Historical stage	Modernity *The third stage*	Traditional *The first phase*
Agent of oppression	Social majority	Political tyranny
Means of oppression	External force	Interior influence

In Mill's view of history, the second stage, the birth of democracy, is the transition between traditional and modern society. In modern times, people are made into the means of their own oppression, the majority tyrannizes as much over its own members as over minorities. In modern times, nobody is free.

Towards the fourth stage: conformity or diversity?

Mill's own theory of liberty is the counter-idea of the tyranny of the majority. His theory is universal but, like Marx's theories, also recognizes its own place in history. These are dangerous times, when progress itself is giving rise to a new tyranny. Neither have things reached their darkest point:

QUOTATION

The majority have not yet learnt to feel the power of the government their power, or its opinions their opinions.

cross reference O: 13; P: 67; N: 47

When the majority becomes truly at home with power, then the new tyranny will begin in earnest. Every exception will be an outrage. The law will be made into the vehicle for suppressing differences.

As yet, the majority has not understood its new role. People retain some of the attitudes of the earlier phase, when the government acted against the will of the majority. Some of the old instincts of ancient liberty still continue. But over time, the people will understand their new status and then there will be an urgent need for a countervailing doctrine of individual liberty. In the next phase, liberty will become the shield of the minority, and the majority will see liberty as their enemy:

Mill's Dialectic of Liberty
Towards a fourth stage

In the future, the majority may identify completely with the state; liberty will appear to them as an enemy.

To the minorities, and the individual who recognizes her or his separateness, liberty will then become the principle of difference.

Unlike Marx, Mill does not see his dialectical view of history as a way to predict the future – but he does hint at different possible futures. Clearly, there is a dark prospect, the fulfilment of the principle of authority under the rule of the majority.

The dark fourth stage: the age of conformity

However, there is also hope. As the dialectic sharpens to its crisis, the concept of liberty reveals its most radical meaning. In the face of universal **conformism**, liberty will be the banner of difference:

QUOTATION
The only freedom which deserves the name is that of pursuing our own good in our own way.
cross reference O: 17; P: 72; N: 50

On the horizon, there is also an age of individuality. In that future, liberty would become the ruling idea of society, and diversity would replace conformity as the social principle.

The bright fourth stage: the age of diversity

The horizon remains open, but there is a utopian possibility implicit in Mill's view of history. Perhaps the struggle will culminate in an era when the individual is truly free to pursue his or her own idea of the good life, for better and worse. In that case, by the dialectic of liberty, the age of conformity will have given birth to a new phase of diversity.

Liberty of the press and the public interest

We now come to the heart of Mill's arguments, Chapter II of *On Liberty*, 'Of the Liberty of Thought and Discussion'. Here he examines **free speech**, one of the most fundamental aspects of modern freedom and one which Mill has most directly influenced. Mill helped to create the agenda of free speech, and his analysis still applies to contemporary controversies where the state, the government, the law or powerful private institutions attempt to constrain public opinion and argument. We will be examining in depth Mill's arguments on freedom of public expression, both in their historical perspective and for their continuing relevance. In this chapter, we focus in close-up on his first case – press freedom – because it is so beautifully argued and so directly relevant.

STEP ONE: PINNING DOWN THE ACCEPTED VIEW

At the start of 'Of the Liberty of Thought and Discussion', Mill offers for his readers' recognition a would-be principle. He calls it, in the terminology of his age and its predecessors, '*the liberty of the press*' (cross reference **O**: 20, **P**: 75, **N**: 52). Presumably, he declares with apparent confidence, no one needs to spend any time nowadays defending or justifying this basic liberty. Everyone accepts that the press must be free, in general, don't they? But what, he adds, just in case anyone has forgotten, is really meant by liberty of the press?

Here Mill begins to give **definitions** and, whenever he does so, you know that the argument is about to take a leap forward – for it is always his aim to unsettle the familiar view of the most important words in public discussion, and to make space for new meanings to emerge. In effect, Mill now applies his dialectical understanding of the history of liberty to a specific case. He is going to show how 'liberty of the press' is an idea from an earlier phase in the historical dialectic of freedom. Unless rethought for the new phase, this once valuable idea will become destructive.

First, then, he defines the inherited understanding of liberty of the press: ' "*liberty of the press*" ... *one of the securities against corrupt or tyrannical government.*' In this respect, it means restraining a government that is not founded upon any democratic or public mandate. No government that is '*not identified in interest with the people*' shall be entitled to '*determine what doctrines*' they can hear. This concept derives from the first phase in the dialectical history of liberty, the phase of the basic struggle between tyrants and the people as a whole, between pure power and society.

STEP ONE
Liberty of the press: accepted definition
The conventional principle: no power or government shall be entitled to regulate the ideas reaching the public if they do not represent that public.

According to Mill, this understanding of press freedom has been passed down to his age by its predecessors. The source of this liberty is really in such events as the Civil War of the seventeenth century, and the religious and political persecutions undertaken by monarchs and their appointed governors. These were the upheavals that brought an end to the first phase of the history of liberty.

This is a typical example of Mill's general technique. He wants to show how the words we inherit belong to the ages from which they come. If we continue to use the language of the past – and no other language is *unthinkingly* available to us – we will automatically repeat the arguments of the past. He has already prepared the ground for a fundamental revision of this key sense of liberty as it applies to public discussion and to ideas. In the current phase of history, the old liberty is out of context. The press no longer needs defending against absolute monarchs.

We are about to begin the journey from the traditional meaning, embodied in the inherited phrase 'liberty of the press', to the modern meaning, which is represented by Mill's 'liberty of thought and discussion'. This is a concept that belongs to the age of the tyranny of the majority – the third phase of the history we saw in the previous chapter. Now power has passed from the tyrants to the people. The old defensive liberty is outdated and a new threat is arising – the third phase where the will of the majority becomes the main threat.

With his usual quiet cunning, Mill has opened a trapdoor under the reader who has accepted with a nod the familiar meaning of liberty. Yes, the press should always be free to include whatever opinions it wants – and no government is entitled to intervene if it does not speak on behalf of the public interest. Mill simply leaves the trap quietly in place. However, if you pause over the argument, you can already see much of the logic of the ensuing discussion. What happens when the government *is* more representative? According to Mill, liberty of the press has been developed as a defence against *unrepresentative* governments, absolute kings and other classical tyrannies. Already by the mid-nineteenth century, there are elections. True, the electorate is narrow, and Mill is one of the principal campaigners for a wider electorate. But the Victorians already have passed the age when the government was simply a hostile force at odds with the interests of society. What will this older principle of liberty mean as government becomes ever more representative of the interest and voice of the public?

STEP TWO: DECONSTRUCTING THE ACCEPTED VIEW

Mill begins to turn the phrase 'liberty of the press' round for our consideration. He reassures us – or appears to – that only in cases of exceptional panic would any modern government try to stifle public debate. Unless faced by an imminent revolution, the enlightened authorities of the nineteenth century will not lapse into the style of past despots. Irony is in the air. This is the next stage of a characteristic Mill argument:

> STEP TWO
> Traditional 'liberty of the press': an ironic perspective
> *In modern times, liberty of the press is assured except in cases of extreme panic or threat to the legitimate order.*

We already have to wonder how far a liberty is real, if a government can choose to revoke it in 'serious' circumstances? Isn't a crisis exactly the moment when public debate is most heated, and most necessary?

Mill now sharpens the irony. The argument enters its second phase, which one can call the **deconstruction** of the inherited meaning of 'liberty of the press'. Mill shows up contradictions within this apparently benign and established word. He is taking us towards a paradox, where the old doctrine of 'liberty of the press' collapses. In a modern society, the old 'liberty' could become a means by which an elected government can actually justify large-scale and frequent censorship. Indeed any authority that can claim to be representative of a public will be able to argue that it leaves opinion absolutely free, *except* when the interests of that public require censorship. The dialectic of history has uprooted the old liberty of the press – it no longer serves to defend the people against the tyrants. Instead, it threatens to reinforce the supposed 'right' of an elected government to restrict public discussion.

Little explosions begin to go off in Mill's apparently peaceful logic. He reassures us that in constitutional countries, by which he means those where some degree of public say is allowed in choosing the government, no authority '*will often attempt to control the expression of opinion.*' There is, it seems, a natural link between political democracy and freedom of discussion. That link, surely, is implicit in the idea that liberty of the press serves the interests of the public at large.

Of course, Mill adds, in a modern society, a government will never suppress opinions or ideas simply out of its own tastes or judgements. No modern government would be so arrogant. On the contrary, a constitutional government will suppress opinions only when it is truly confident that it is acting as:

KEY QUOTE
...the organ of the general intolerance of the public.
cross reference O: 21; P: 76; N: 53

Anatomy of the Key Quote

- '*general intolerance*': Toleration is the original founding concept of liberal philosophy and practice. Toleration begins as the argument against religious persecution, and becomes a more general approach to differing values and ways of life. The enemy of the liberal, therefore, was religious persecution, and is now its descendant, the spirit of intolerance. We can see the same antagonism in the very different liberalism of Mill's contemporary, Matthew Arnold.

- '*the public*': The whole concept of 'the public' is born with the age of democracy. The public is the collective spirit. The majority acts as the public when seeking to suppress all minorities and eccentrics. The public is a majority that refuses to acknowledge any exceptions.

- In other words, if liberty of the press means the right to express any view, which *the public wants to hear*, then a government that really represents that public – its interest – will have the right, even the duty, to suppress those views which the public is quite unanimous about not wanting to hear.

The old liberty is inadequate for a changing world. There was a time when it was enough to found liberty of the press upon the right of the public to hear those ideas *which it wished* to hear. That was when the enemy of free discussion was absolute monarchy, acting without regard to the public interest, indeed habitually acting against that public interest. But as government comes under the sway – formally and informally – of public opinion, then this old version of liberty will no longer protect free debate. Now Mill is beginning to set up a contrast between the old version of liberty and his own new Legitimacy Test – that interference is only to be justified on grounds of actual harm.

Mill unfolds a darkening future: **democracy without freedom**. In a democratic age, even a half or quarter democratic age, a new theory of liberty will be necessary. The old principles – freedom for the people – will simply serve to strengthen any authority that represents the public, or society. You can actually *feel* the word liberty slipping loose from past meanings. Mill is a master of this quiet deconstruction: a familiar word softly implodes. In the space, Mill prepares a new meaning of 'liberty': after the deconstruction, there will be a reconstruction, which carries on for the rest of *On Liberty* – '*the reconstruction of liberty as a restraint on the will of the majority.*'

Mill has shown us why traditional doctrines of liberty will not keep a democracy free. Liberty of the press is meant to be the phrase that safeguards the freedom of public discussion, the widest possible communication of ideas and arguments but, Mill shows, the unthinking use of the phrase will have the reverse effect. Liberty of the press could even become the cornerstone of a doctrine of control and limitation, a founding principle of a democratic form of censorship. This will happen if liberty continues to be understood as defined by public interest or opinion, or by the rights of a legitimately representative government.

STEP TWO
Traditional 'liberty of the press': a deconstruction
No government will be entitled to suppress public discussion of an opinion or idea unless:

* *that government is acting fully as the 'voice' of the public, or in accordance with public interest;*

* *there is extreme danger to the legitimate order.*

In effect, therefore, we have reached a paradox: the goal of Mill's ironic method of defining accepted terms. The better a government is, in the sense of being representative of public opinion, the worse it might become, in the sense of feeling justified in suppressing unwanted ideas. There is nothing in the unthinking version of liberty of the press to prevent such a government from suppressing any ideas that annoy its public. It will permit absolute freedom except when its 'coercion' harmonizes with the public interest and articulates 'agreement' with the public 'voice'. The old liberty becomes the basis for a new tyranny.

Traditional 'liberty of the press': an impossible paradox
The more closely a government or authority represents the public and voices its opinion, the more entitled it is to suppress the expression of unwanted opinions or ideas.

The same idea of liberty, which was revolutionary in one age, could support oppression in the next. This is the dialectical insight implicit in the critical, or deconstructive phase of Mill's argument, an insight with implications far beyond the specific cases and contexts under discussion in his text.

MILL IN THE TWENTY-FIRST CENTURY

Mill has now prepared the ground for his wider argument about free speech and thought. Clearly he is going to argue the need for a different account of liberty, one that makes it more difficult for modern governments and the public to suppress unpopular views and voices. However, before we follow those arguments, it is worthwhile considering the continuing relevance of his specific analysis of the doctrine of liberty of the press with reference to contemporary relations between government and the media. How does our time fare in relation to Mill's Liberal Legitimacy Test?

When you look at the detail, you might think that Mill's arguments have dated, that he is addressing issues of the mid-nineteenth century. It is certainly important to recognize the degree to which *On Liberty* belongs to its age. Mill is arguing about the prospects for democracy; we are living in the aftermath of those arguments. The time before any meaningful elections at all is still close at hand for Mill, and the memory of the struggle between society and absolute monarchy is still fresh. Nevertheless, his approach is still directly relevant in a number of ways.

Democratic censorship in the twenty-first century

One of the main ways in which a modern government regulates and restricts public debate is through its control of **access to information**. Clearly if information is not available, discussion is limited or impossible. So one of the most powerful means of censorship is the withholding of information – much of which is either directly or indirectly under government control. The government's authority for controlling this information flow derives directly from its democratic mandate. As our representative, the government is entitled to decide where to limit access to information, if there are grounds for thinking it might have a disastrous effect on the public interest. An example might be research on a safety issue, where release of data might cause undue panic, or economic crisis, and where there is still a specialist debate.

Another example might be information about disagreements between ministers and officials; or release of data that would help terrorists or military opponents.

In the UK this problem has given rise to a continuing debate about **freedom of information**. In 1994, the then Conservative government introduced a code of openness – the central principle being that the grounds for withholding information were primarily based on a '**test of harm**'. In effect, this applied the language of Mill's Legitimacy Test, or Harm Criterion. But this language proved too strong for respectable governments and politicians on the eve of the third millennium!

There has been a continuing campaign for wider measures to ensure access to information, and the campaigners have argued for the consistent and legally binding application of this 'test of harm'. Mill had argued that the only ground for limiting liberty was 'harm' – now the campaigners argued that where no such harm was evident, information should automatically flow into the public domain.

In 1998, the New Labour Government of Tony Blair drew up a plan, involving a freedom of information commissioner, with the power to require an authority to consider revealing information 'in the public interest' – but not the power to enforce that release of information.

Jack Straw, the minister responsible, saw a great widening of access to information, and so of free debate:

QUOTATION
...the bill requires an authority to consider disclosing information, *taking into account all the circumstances of the case,* including the public interest.

[Author's emphases]

Critics replied acerbically that: '*Ministers would decide **if it is in the public interest** to reveal information.*' This is the core issue. *Who* decides on 'the public interest'? The Government argued that it must be responsible for regulating the flow of information, and hence of discussion: '*to leave these decisions to the Information Commissioner would be "profoundly undemocratic".*'

The argument is precisely the one Mill anticipated in his 1859 discussion. The government is democratically elected, and so it has the right to decide on the limits of public freedom of discussion. Indeed, the government is acting here on behalf of the public. We have here an example of Mill's history of freedom. An inherited understanding of liberty is now out of context. In the new phase, the old concept backfires.

Already in 1859, Mill was arguing that democracy could become the basis for a resurgence of censorship of public discussion. The old concepts of liberty had arisen in protest at traditional tyranny by kings or aristocrats. Why shouldn't a publicly elected regime restrict discussion in line with its popular mandate? Why shouldn't ministers decide what is in the public interest to reveal, subject to appropriate checks and scrutiny? For example, would it really be in the public interest to know the details of reports on possible petrol shortages before they became truly relevant? Wouldn't that simply cause panic and trigger a crisis? Would it be in the public interest to reveal sensitive debates about the handling of peace negotiations, say in Northern Ireland?

Yet all such information has, in effect, the potential for a discussion. In restricting the information, a twenty-first-century government is limiting public debate just as surely as any earlier regime, though with less brutality. Mill does not give a simple yes/no answer to any specific question. You can't discover in *On Liberty* the recipe for deciding whether specific data about a remote risk to public health should be released while the experts remain divided. However, Mill encourages a state of mind which is sceptical towards official justifications of censorship, including censorship by data management.

Mill's classic analysis of liberty of the press looks back to the seventeenth century, and points forward into the twenty-first century.

5 Hearing the arguments

Now we examine Mill's arguments on 'liberty of thought and discussion' throughout the main body of his second chapter. Throughout the analysis, we are going to see how Mill cuts away, one after another, the reasons which seem to justify restricting liberty of thought and discussion. The whole chapter is a process of elimination. We are left with his own principle of liberty, the Harm Criterion.

This method produces a distinctive intellectual excitement. Mill's own reasoning enacts his belief in the need for the collision of ideas. In his other works, Mill was also a leading theorist of logic, and the second chapter of *On Liberty* is a great example of Mill's own art of thinking, which one might also call 'the art of seeing ideas whole'.

MILL'S ART OF THINKING

* *The method of reasonable extremism.* Mill demands that we take the whole of an argument through to its conclusion and do not stop short where it seems 'sensible' to us.

* *The dialectical approach to ideas.* Mill requires us to see each idea from as many points of view as possible, including as many hostile points of view as possible. Thinking is the art of taking into account every possible objection.

If we do not follow an argument as far as it can go, and if we do not entertain every serious objection, then we cannot be said to have understood that argument. This is a demanding standard of reasoning, and Mill's own practice is its greatest defence.

Throughout his argument, Mill will be demanding that we listen to the views of those who seem to us offensive, destructive, wrong, mad, cranky and irrelevant. The argument has a human core. To illustrate we will be bringing in a few modern character types.

Purist

A *purist* will never compromise. He or she has the key to life, the answer to every problem. Other people usually assume that 'Purist' is a kind of irrelevance. Do we really need to listen? Can't we just, in the most polite way, delete this tiresome and obsessive viewpoint from public debate?

Extremist

An *extremist* is drawn to take up exactly the position that is most offensive to everyone else. Whatever the mainstream view, 'Extremist' will be found proclaiming the reverse. He or she will never use a mild word where an abusive one is available. The mark of an extremist is that he or she assumes an argument is good when everyone is offended or outraged.

Paranoiac

A *paranoiac* believes there is a plot at work. Everyone else is deceived but he or she knows the hidden secret. 'Paranoiac' tends to focus on a single issue or explanation. To the mainstream eye, Paranoiac is the least rational of all these outsiders.

Mill's argument is effectively written as a dialogue, though he does not give the other side a name. We might call this adversary 'Normal', the voice of a commonsense which cannot imagine the need for any other views or voices. Normal generally suggests that we do not need to hear from such types as Purist, Extremist and Paranoiac – that their voices mess up proper discussion and distort public debate. They poison the atmosphere, they distract attention from the real issues and they are anyway impossible to argue with. Of course, we may not believe in locking them up – though sometimes we might – but we know there are many other ways to keep such voices silent, at least as far as public discussion is concerned.

In his argument, Mill imagines a number of arguments that a Normal type might use against free discussion:

* *The Unanimity Argument*: 'But everyone else agrees!'

* *The Absurdity Argument*: 'I won't listen to this nonsense!'

* *The Offended Argument*: 'But that's outrageous!'

* *The Threatened Argument*: 'That idea threatens the foundations of decent society!'

* *The Confident Argument*: 'But we already know the truth!'

Against these propositions, Mill argues not only that we should tolerate dissenting characters and weird ideas in our public life – but also that we absolutely need them.

THE UNANIMITY ARGUMENT: 'BUT EVERYONE ELSE AGREES!'

To Normal, it seems obvious that where everyone agrees, there is no need to tolerate futile objections. Free discussion has its limits, and one of them is where society has made up its mind. Mill replies on behalf of all extremists, purists, paranoiacs and other exceptions:

KEY QUOTE

If all mankind minus one were of one opinion, mankind would be no more justified in silencing that person than he, if he had the power, would be justified in silencing mankind.

cross reference O: 21; P: 76; N: 53

Anatomy of the Key Quote

o *'minus one'*: **For Mill, the reasonable extremist, the exception has equal weight with the rule.**

o *'of one opinion'*: **That would-be unanimity is the ideal form of public opinion. This state is the goal of every 'public'.**

Take the case of 'the Last Marxist', a contemporary form of purist. Let's say nobody else believes in Marxist principles any more. We all think the Cold War was won 20 years ago. Do we really have to listen to this voice, endlessly explaining why the Class War is still going on, why imperialism is the cause of world poverty? Can't society simply refuse to invite the Last Marxist along to the party? He can simply be left off all the agendas, kept away from every episode of *Question Time*, turned away from all publishers' lists and so on. This in Mill's terms is absolutely wrong. We are no more entitled to shut the Last Marxist up than he or she is to silence the rest of the world.

Here we can see Mill drawing simultaneously on the Liberal Legitimacy Test and the Appeal to Utility. If the exception does no harm, the rest of mankind is not entitled to suppress his voice: that is the logical consequence of flowing through the Harm Criterion. The appeal to utility adds a positive angle:

KEY QUOTE

But the peculiar evil of silencing an opinion is, that it is robbing the human race, posterity as well as the existing generation – those who dissent from the opinion still more than those who hold it.

cross reference O: 21; P: 76; N: 53

Anatomy of the Key Quote

o '… *robbing the human race*': This is probably the single most important phrase in Mill's defence of freedom of thought and discussion. If we decide to keep a voice quiet, then we are damaging the interests of the whole of humanity.

o '*posterity as well as the existing generation*': Mill defined utility as 'the permanent interests' of humanity as a 'progressive' species. Here he applies that standard positively: ideas are forever, censorship violates the rights of the future to decide for itself!

Take an example. For many of us, one of the most boring forms of 'extremist' is 'the only man', the Last True Male. Would pushing the off switch on this voice really be robbing humanity? Do we need to give airtime to his brilliant discoveries that masculinity has been betrayed, or that he alone has the right to whatever he wants? According to Mill, humanity does need this voice, as it needs every other voice: '*If the opinion is right*' then we have lost out on an opportunity to discover the truth. But more important, if the opinion is wrong:

KEY QUOTE

…they lose, what is almost as great a benefit, the clearer perception and livelier impression of truth produced by its collision with error.

cross reference O: 21; P: 76; N: 53

Anatomy of the Key Quote

o '*its collision*': This is a clear statement of dialectic. Ideas need their opposites to flourish.

o '*benefit*': The terms 'benefit' and 'cost' have become central to the analysis and assessment of welfare.

○ '*impression*': This term has a long history in English philosophy and poetry, including Wordsworth, Mill's much-loved romantic poet. An impression is the subjective impact of the moment of perception.

THE ABSURDITY ARGUMENT: 'I WON'T LISTEN TO THIS NONSENSE!'

Normal has plenty of other arguments against free discussion. Why should someone sensible have to put up with the intrusion of views that are patently ridiculous? This is the Absurdity Argument, a common alternative to the Unanimity argument. Mill replies with his own brand of extremist reasoning!

QUOTATION

We can never be sure that the opinion we are endeavouring to stifle is a false opinion.

cross reference O: 22; P: 76; N: 54

This is a strong view, which goes a lot further than most people would follow. Normal, and his or her philosophical representatives, would ask: Can we really never be sure that an opinion is false?

Take Paranoiac at his or her most extravagant. There are plenty of contemporary examples. For instance, Paranoiac believes that the United Nations is trying to take over America, or that baby food is being sold which is known to be unsafe. The problem is that sometimes Paranoiac does seem to hit the target and the mainstream then looks complacent or worse. Mill isn't saying that Paranoiac is likely to be right. He is allowing a space.

Answering the Absurdity Argument, Mill comes up with a classic statement:

> **KEY QUOTE**
> *All silencing of discussion is an assumption of infallibility.*
> cross reference O: 22; P: 77; N: 54

Anatomy of the Key Quote

o '*infallibility*': This key word has a long history in religious and political conflict going back to the Protestant reformation and the Catholic view of papal authority. The Pope took upon himself the status of being infallible, with regard to religious doctrine. Protestantism was born partly in reaction to this notion of papal infallibility. But Mill insists it is common for people to assume they are infallible without realizing it. '*Every time you keep someone else out of the discussion, you are effectively assuming that you are infallible.*'

o '*assumption*': One of the functions of modern logic is to reveal and discredit the hidden assumptions of ordinary arguments. Mill-the-logician is the enemy of the latent assumption.

In effect, Mill is applying his Liberal Legitimacy Test to the would-be censors. Even if an idea is absurd, what harm is it doing? He is also resorting, perhaps more forcefully, to the Utility Appeal:

> **QUOTATION**
> *...the opinion which it is attempted to suppress by authority may possibly be true. Those who desire to suppress it, of course deny its truth; but they are not infallible.*
> cross reference O: ??; P: ??; N: ??

This argument is subtler than it looks. At first glance, one thinks: this is 'liberal relativism', that is, the view that there is no absolute truth, only different points of view. We have to accept other points of view, because there *are only viewpoints*. There is no such thing as the truth; therefore everyone gets to put a point of view. In fact, Mill is not that kind of liberal at all. His objection to would-be infallibility is founded on his love of truth, not on mere acceptance of different viewpoints. He takes truth extremely seriously. It is because we are trying genuinely to get closer to the truth about an issue, that we cannot afford to rule out of court any arguments in advance.

The truth may be a limit towards which we reach but which we never attain – but the journey is still serious. It is a sign of our good faith in any discussion, our commitment to finding the truth out, that we let all the voices join in, even the ones which seem to us most far-fetched, most offensive, most destructive.

Here Mill is doing far more than object to censorship. He is also making a positive case. We could say that he is establishing the standards for genuine discussion, and so for an authentic public culture, but Mill allows the other side to object, what about ideas that are 'dangerous' as well as absurd? After all, the two may go together, from a normal perspective. Are there not, he asks on behalf of his critics, some views that are '*dangerous to the welfare of mankind, either in this life or another*'? In that case, the Utility appeal would work the other way round, as a basis for censorship.

The medical panic: a fictional scenario

Take, in our time, a group of Paranoiac Extremists, who combine the wild obsession of the one with the deliberate offensiveness of the other. They go around arguing that modern medicine is a vast conspiracy. It is not safe to give any medical treatment, and particularly not to children. They begin to make headway. Worried parents are keeping their children away from clinics and doctors on an increasing scale. There are signs that this is causing the beginning of a serious epidemic and deterioration in infant mortality figures. Is there not a strong case for trying to silence these views, for the good of the children?

Every expert agrees that this panic is based on lies, distortions and misconceptions. Does the government not have a duty to try to suppress this panic-inducing campaign? Perhaps there should be a new charge of falsely inducing public panic? Or maybe there should be simply a concerted campaign of vilification against this group? Perhaps the media should refrain from giving them space? Mill would insist that we have to face out the argument, even with these Paranoiac Extremists. Of course, if they start attacking clinics, or sending letter bombs to doctors, then they have violated the liberty of others and they fall foul of the Harm Criterion. But if they are genuinely arguing their 'mad' case, we have to meet them on that ground. The reason is that somewhere in their chaotic rant, there may be something true, something neglected. Alternatively, we may discover the true basis for our faith in medical treatment more clearly by refuting them.

The BSE scandal: a historical scenario

In reply, you might say, that is a fantasy case: it illustrates the ideas in theory, but in practice we are too grown up to censor silly arguments on the grounds that they are dangerous. However, there are many different versions of 'silencing' and some of them do seem to play a part in the regulation of our public debates.

Take a current case: the BSE controversy. This is a classic illustration of Mill's main points: first, that society is always keen to silence awkward views; second, that there are many ways of silencing unwanted viewpoints; and third, that one can never be sure that what seems to be a marginal and extreme view will not turn out to have weight, even in an apparently scientific issue. When the first voices were raised in the UK about the spread of infection to humans, they were generally treated with contempt. There were cases where experts lost grants, or were threatened with the loss of their jobs, or actually lost their jobs. The media coverage of these 'prophets of doom' was mocking or worse. All of these are examples of modern censorship – our ways to silence then unwanted argument. This case also illustrates vividly Mill's positive point, for here it did indeed turn out that some at least of the far-fetched claims needed to be taken seriously. Such examples illustrate Mill's argument that utility and liberty are inseparable. Free discussion is in the interests of mankind.

THE OFFENDED ARGUMENT: 'BUT THAT'S OUTRAGEOUS!'

There are plenty of other 'Normal' arguments for censoring free discussion. The most heated of all is the 'Offended Argument'. This is where someone, speaking for the mainstream, declares that an individual or a minority is offending their deepest sensibilities.

Mill is not going to argue merely for tolerating offensive views, he insists that we should actually welcome and even encourage them. In the end, the argument focuses on religious and moral blasphemy. To explain his approach, he starts with a 'cool' example:

KEY QUOTE

If even the Newtonian philosophy were not permitted to be questioned, mankind could not feel as complete assurance of its truth as they now do.

cross reference O: 26; P: 81; N: 57

Anatomy of the Key Quote

o *'the Newtonian philosophy'*: Newton's Laws of Motion had been scientific gospel since the seventeenth century and include the Law of Gravity. In this argument, though, the 'Newtonian philosophy' stands for any Great Truth, which has worked its way into the whole outlook of a society.

o *'even'*: This is not really an argument about gravity. The word
'even' turns this example into a kind of 'limit case'. What Mill
means is that society considers it unacceptable to question other
kinds of Great Truth which, by implication, are less secure than
the Newtonian philosophy.

The more important a Great Truth seems, the more essential it is to
allow others to challenge it. The reason is that if nobody ever denies
'even' the law of gravity, it will cease to have any real meaning. We
will stop thinking about it. Mill then gives the example of the
Catholic Church that arranges for a devil's advocate to argue against
the canonization of any new proposed saint. Every Great Truth
should have an equivalent role.

Mill now introduces into the argument the important term,
'extreme', and gives a defence of the need to apply freedom to what
are seen as the most extreme views at any given time. Here he is
taking on, face to face, the 'Offended Argument' for censorship:

KEY QUOTE

*Strange it is that men should admit the validity of the
arguments for free discussion, but object to their being
'pushed to an extreme', not seeing that unless the reasons
are good for an extreme case, they are not good for
any case.*

cross reference O: 26; P: 81; N: 57

Anatomy of the Key Quote

o *'admit the validity'*: People are reluctant to accept the basis for
uncensored expression. There is a sense of working against the
grain throughout this section of *On Liberty*.

o *'an extreme'*: People want to keep a 'sensible' limit on free
discussion, even though they have no valid argument for doing

so. 'Extreme', here, indicates that Mill is moving on to consider those ideas and viewpoints that strike the mainstream as too outrageous, as offensive in their very existence.

So Mill insists that if a society is serious about free discussion, it will actively encourage the most unacceptable views to be expressed openly and clearly. He confronts our Normal face to face. For Normal there are certain values that are beyond challenge. To doubt them is to commit a sin: *'none but bad men would desire to weaken these salutary beliefs'* (cross reference **O**: 27; **P**: 82; **N**: 58).

In our time, such Great Truths might include 'family values' or 'work is good for you'. Consider the abusive representation of those who challenge family values – an abuse which Mill would count as a form of censorship. In this context, Mill uses blasphemy and heresy as positive terms: they represent challenges to established assumptions, without which there is no scope for change. He then turns to religious examples of offensive views:

QUOTATION

Let the opinions impugned be the belief in a God and in a future state, or any of the commonly received doctrines of morality.

cross reference **O**: 28; **P**: 83; **N**: 58

God and morality go together. Is it simply morally unacceptable to question these sacred beliefs? Sacred beliefs are really the fertile ground for Extremist. You cannot think of a cherished belief that will not attract critical invective. Certainly this is likely to get pretty offensive to the believers, whether in God or in the family or in heterosexual decency. But after all, who counts as an extremist may change depending on the perspective. The first great philosopher, Socrates, was put to death for subverting the established moral beliefs of Athens. *'Mankind can hardly be too often reminded that there was once a man called Socrates'* (cross reference **O**: 29; **P**; 84; **N**: 59).

More contentiously, there is the case of Jesus himself:

QUOTATION

The man who left on the memory of those who witnessed his life and conversation, such an impression of his moral grandeur that eighteen subsequent centuries have done homage to him as the Almighty in person, was ignominiously put to death, as what? As a blasphemer.

cross reference O: 30; P: 85; N: 60

Here Mill is deepening his defence of blasphemy as possessing positive utility. If we look beyond the present moment, if we see the vista of history, then we realize we cannot be sure how a person or his views will appear. There seems to be reason to think that the most creative figures in history will strike their own time as blasphemous. Precisely those views that lead to real change and advancement, will be most offensive to their own day. How could it be otherwise?

Here again the basis for the defence of liberty is a dialectical view of history. We need counter-ideas to oppose the present orthodoxy, otherwise humanity will be frozen. We cannot take it upon ourselves to decide which extremist in our day will turn out to be the herald of human progress, and which will be a mere nuisance. In fact, it is probably true that most times Extremist is just a pain. The trouble is, occasionally he or she is the new age calling.

The Offended Argument for censorship is one of the most dangerous. First, Mill insists, cutting out Extremists violates the Liberal Legitimacy Test. They are doing no 'harm to others', except for upsetting the mainstream. Second, and more importantly, Mill applies his Appeal to Utility. Extremism may turn out to be in the long-term interests of the growth of the human race. Nobody can be sure at the time whether this particular outrageous view will turn out to have such historical utility.

THE THREATENED ARGUMENT: 'THAT IDEA THREATENS THE FOUNDATIONS OF DECENT SOCIETY!'

Are any values necessary for the survival of society? Here the Victorian critic James Stephen was particularly outraged: obviously, he proclaimed, society must protect its basic values from attack! For Mill, this question follows from the previous discussion of heretics. For example, Mill recalls, the Roman Emperor Marcus Aurelius suppressed Christianity because he believed it would undermine decent Roman society:

> KEY QUOTE
>
> *... he saw, or thought he saw that it [society] was held together, and prevented from being worse, by belief and reverence of the received divinities.*
>
> cross reference O: 31; P: 86; N: 61

Anatomy of the Key Quote

o *'held together ... by belief'*: This is a common assumption: that certain beliefs glue society together. Where these beliefs are concerned, social unity takes precedence over liberty.

o *'the received divinities'*: In Roman times, the pagan gods presided over the central institutions of society. Mill is being satirical. In later times, there are different founding dogmas: the nation, the monarchy.

Marcus Aurelius was a decent man and a genuine philosopher. However, he is an enemy of liberty because he denied freedom to an ideology that 'openly aimed at dissolving ties'. This is the Threatened Argument for censorship. Certain ideas are too subversive. Society is too fragile to permit absolutely free discussion.

Mill's attack on this Threatened Argument follows on from his defence of heretics against mainstream outrage. In the main, the subversives have been people of good faith. They know that as dissidents they must preserve a higher standard of decency in order not to discredit their ideas in the eyes of the mainstream:

QUOTATION

…it is historically true that a large portion of infidels in all ages have been persons of distinguished integrity and honour.

cross reference O: 21; P: 76; N: 53

The Threatened Argument works by instilling fear, both in the majority and in the dissidents. We are standing on the brink of social collapse; let's all cling together and hang on to the beliefs that keep us safe. In that oppressive atmosphere, minorities fall silent and keep their views to themselves:

KEY QUOTE

Those in whose eyes this reticence on the part of heretics is no evil should consider … that in consequence of it there is never any fair and thorough discussion of heretical opinions.

cross reference O: 38; P: 95; N: 66

Anatomy of the Key Quote

o '*reticence*': Merely making people hesitate to speak is enough to suppress free discussion. All censorship is total censorship.

o '*fair and thorough*': Only in a free discussion can the heresy be refuted. If the outsiders aren't refuted, they will never learn. If we don't try to refute them, we will never learn the limits of the mainstream.

Two key points emerge from Mill's discussion of social coherence and freedom.

1 There is no such thing as a partly free discussion.

2 There is never a case for the utility of suppressing a viewpoint. The Threatened Argument for censorship suggests that society as a whole may be better off if certain views are kept silent. Mill, however, replies that the effect is a loss of well-being on both sides – censors and censored.

THE CONFIDENT ARGUMENT: 'BUT WE ALREADY KNOW THE TRUTH!'

Surely if what 'we' say is true, there is no need for us to listen to the other side? Mill goes to work by successive arguments to undermine this apparently plausible and commonsensical position. He comes up with a series of vivid formulations to make us look again at the very words 'true' and 'truth':

> QUOTATION
>
> *Popular opinions … are often true, but seldom or never the whole truth. Heretical opinions … are generally some of these suppressed and neglected truths.*
>
> cross reference O: 52; P: 108; N: 76

Mill's argument is about truth and history.

* Heresy is often the other side of truth, the side unseen by a particular period.

* The truth is dialectical: it consists of the endless play of oppositions. To limit that play is to block the path to illumination.

Heresy is, Mill insists, often the more urgent side of the truth for any given period. The familiar aspect of truth is liable to be less helpful than the one we have been avoiding: '*The new fragment of truth is more wanted, more adapted to the needs of the time than that which it displaces.*'

Mill seeks to confront us with the sheer scale of the truth, as a field far larger than conventional thinking has assumed. His argument is comparable with nineteenth-century discoveries about time. Previously, time had been thought of on a more or less human scale: the earth and the universe belonged to a humanly comprehensible story. However, Victorian geology and biology replaced this narrow view of time with a sense of 'deep time' – notably in Darwin's *Origin of Species*. Mill is arguing for a similar revision in the understanding of truth, a sense of how deep and broad the truth must be, how far it extends in all directions beyond our ordinary beliefs and ideas.

Mill devotes a specific discussion to Christian ethics. They are valid, but incomplete. Originally, it was Christianity that expressed a necessary heresy, the side of ethical truth hidden from classical ethics, which insisted on service to society and overlooked personal salvation: '*Christian ethics ... they contain, and were meant to contain, only a part of the truth.*'

We tend to think of ethics as a matter of opinion, but Mill thinks of different ethical systems as contributions to a dialectical argument about truth. In this regard, his thinking resembles that of another great Victorian liberal, Matthew Arnold, who proposed a famous division between Hebraic and Hellenic systems.

Mill ends this ethical argument by insisting that his goal is '*the mental well-being of mankind*'. Well-being is the main theme in his next chapter.

Free to be human: Mill's proverbs of well-being

Chapter III of *On Liberty* is called 'Of Individuality'. In this section of the guide, we shall see how, for Mill, individuality is the bedrock of the argument about freedom. Every argument stops somewhere, – where, as the contemporary philosopher Hilary Putnam says, the spade eventually touches the bedrock. Even the most sophisticated chain of reasoning has an ending, a point beyond which the reasons will not take you. In Mill's case, that resting point is 'individuality'. If you ask, what is the point of freedom?, the answer at the end of the chain of reasons is: freedom enables us to be individuals, to be ourselves.

We can see that Mill has reached a different phase of his argument, because he adopts a new style. In his earlier chapters, he writes in a reasoning voice which:

* makes connections between ideas;

* answers objections to ideas.

Now another voice enters, or becomes more audible. This is a **proverbial voice**. The third chapter is full of sayings or near-sayings. In some ways, the writing is more like a reasonable-seeming version of Oscar Wilde than a 'normal philosopher'. Why does Mill speak in this proverbial voice? He has reached some end-points in his reasoning. These are not arbitrary claims, they are still linked to reasons, but they are also where the reasons come to rest. These sayings are reason's points of homecoming. Therefore, Mill naturally expresses such ideas in a more final-sounding style. At the same time, the sayings are also provocative. Though understated, the proverbs are in their way as outrageous, for conventional opinion, as anything in Wilde or Nietzsche.

INDIVIDUALITY AND WELL-BEING

Consider first the full chapter heading: '*Of Individiduality, as One of the Elements of Well-Being*'. Mill is not, in the end, going to defend individuality on moral or political grounds. The whole argument culminates in a theory of human well-being.

> The grounds of freedom
> *Liberty permits individuality. Without individuality, there is no well-being.*

There is a clear line of reasoning. Without liberty, we cannot be ourselves, or even find out where to look for our true selves. Well-being consists of being yourself, as fully as possible. Who would argue against well-being? According to Mill, most conventional values violate human well-being because they attempt to suppress the expression of individuality. Most people hold moralistic views of the human condition, which demand that people conform to some externally fixed standard or criterion of the good life, the best way of living. *On Liberty* now conducts an intellectual war against that moralistic paradigm.

Mill's view of freedom is still radical because it sweeps aside moralistic thinking, on behalf of the bedrock notion of human well-being. No one is entitled to tell you what makes for your own individual well-being. By '**individuality**', therefore, Mill means the reverse of conformity. We have seen in the previous chapter, how his defence of free discussion is based upon the argument for diversity. We need as many different ideas and arguments as possible for a healthy society. Only through conflict and contrast does intellectual progress occur. The truth itself leaves space for different and conflicting ideas. Now he extends the same dialectical outlook to his treatment of individual lives.

The logic of liberty
If individuality produces well-being, then conformity is bad for you.

Throughout, we have raised the question of Mill's utilitarian theory and how it relates to his argument about liberty. In his treatment of individuality, Mill is both an advocate of liberty and a utilitarian. Well-being is a more subtle and humane version of the utilitarian concept of happiness. Freedom is good because it enhances well-being and therefore is useful, in this philosophical sense of spreading genuine happiness, relieving genuine frustration.

In what follows, we pick out the key sayings that are scattered through this great chapter on individual well-being, as if they made up a 'dictionary of well-being'.

MILL'S PROVERBS OF WELL-BEING

QUOTATION

THE FIRST PROVERB OF WELL-BEING

Men should be free to act upon their opinions

cross reference O: 62; P: 119; N: 84

Mill's Dictionary of Well-Being

o '*Being free*' means that you can act upon your opinions. It is not enough to be able to hold or even express an opinion, if you are prevented from acting on it. Therefore, freedom of opinion includes being able to act.

o '*Freedom to*' is as important as 'freedom from'. In fact, you could say that 'freedom to' is the point, the pay-off of 'freedom from'. Being free from interference is the negative half of being free to act. This proverb of well-being is about 'freedom to' – the preceding arguments about public discussion focused on 'freedom from'.

○ '*Their opinions*': A person cannot truly be said to hold their own opinions if they cannot express them in practice. This is the full meaning of opinion.

Implications

Authentication

An opinion is not authentic if the holder is not able to act on it. Mill is a rational thinker and one tends to associate authenticity with more romantic spirits, say, Nietzsche or D. H. Lawrence. However, as we have seen, Mill is very much an advocate of authenticity. You could see this as part of the Victorian intellectuals' opposition to what they saw as the hypocrisy of their age. If people are forbidden to act on their opinion, then they are effectively turned into hypocrites. After a time, such a society will produce people who do not know whether they are sincere or not, whether they really believe an opinion or are just playing.

The science of opinion

This proverb also has a scientific aspect. If you cannot act on your opinions, it is like a science that is restricted to mere hypotheses – you will never test them. In effect, opinions are moral hypotheses or psychological hypotheses or political hypotheses. Acts are the experiments that test these hypotheses. If I cannot act on my opinion, I am being deprived, too, of the opportunity to refute it.

Qualifications

Mill qualifies this proverb in two ways:

1 *Positively*. The obstacles to this freedom of action are twofold: physical or moral. We need to be free from both these hindrances if we are truly to lay down the foundations for our own lives. Morality is no different from physical restraint. This negative morality is simply a way of restricting the lives of others. Morality becomes a prison-house.

2 *Negatively.* Mill adds that people are free to act on their opinion 'at their own risk'. This links him with a strong current in contemporary social and ethical thought, where 'risk' has become a central topic. For Mill, risk is integral to freedom. A free person can take chances with his or her own life. If you are not allowed to take risks, then you are not an autonomous individual: that is one of the dividing lines between children and adults.

A free society cannot remove risk from the lives of its citizens. Without risks, there can be no individuality. Society cannot make people lead safe lives.

QUOTATION

THE SECOND PROVERB OF WELL-BEING

while mankind are imperfect ... there should be different experiments of living

cross reference O: 63; P: 120; N: 84

Mill's Dictionary of Well-Being

o '*Imperfect*': There is a characteristic irony: will mankind ever be anything else? But the point is also a serious one: humanity evolves and we may approach closer to perfection than we are at present. Either way, mankind will need variety: that is the source of change.

o '*Experiments*': It is as if our lives are scientific projects. Each genuinely free individual makes his or her own hypothesis about the good life. Such lives are like scientific experiments: they test out a theory in practice. Just as science eliminates errors and makes new discoveries through such testing, so our practical knowledge also advances. 'Experimental' also implies something new, something original: there is a link with the previous idea of 'risk'.

Implications

In a free society, there is a dialectic of life choices, a contest between contrasting life visions. Each person makes his or her own life choice and then there is effectively a competition between these alternatives. This contest serves a purpose in the historical development of humanity. Over time, it emerges that this choice is productive, that one is flawed. Mill talks about these experiments as being 'useful': he is applying utility' to the question of individual choice. Humanity as a whole will benefit if individuals are free to experiment with their lives. Though each person may gain or lose, mankind as a whole will be better off. Cumulatively, there will be more well-being in the world, if people are allowed to test out alternative lifestyles.

History is the only legitimate judge of the value of a life choice. Has that way of living proved beneficial to humanity?

QUOTATION

THE THIRD PROVERB OF WELL-BEING

it is the privilege and proper condition of a human being ... to use and interpret experience in his own way

cross reference O: 64; P: 122; N: 86

Mill's Dictionary of Well-Being

o '*The privilege and proper condition*': **Mill does not invoke the idea of 'rights' in his argument for freedom. He does not argue that we have a human right to be free, but he does see humanity as having a 'proper condition', which is defined by liberty. The word condition is originally medical: to be in good condition means to be healthy. This right condition is a part of our human well-being. Though we don't have rights, in Mill's argument, our human nature can only express itself in certain environments.**

The word 'privilege' feels ironic in this context. Nobody grants us the privilege of our humanity: it is simply ours by nature.

o 'Interpret': Interpretation is a central theme of modern thought. For example, it is the theme of Freud's theories, which begin with his *Interpretation of Dreams*. We make life our own by giving it our meaning. Interpretation turns what happens to me into *my* experience. Through interpretation, we live life from the inside. Meaning gives the 'mine-ness' to my life. Mill couples 'interpret' with 'use': there is nothing fanciful or abstract about interpretation. If we cannot give meaning to our lives, we are unable to make use of them.

Implications

If human beings interpret their own lives, they are being 'reflexive'. Mill is arguing that our liberty includes the scope to be fully self-reflexive. This links him with later thinkers, including some of the most influential in our time, notably the sociologist Anthony Giddens and the theorist of 'risk society', Ulrich Beck.

No wonder Mill's reputation is on the rise. These are the criteria of postmodern liberty. In this theory of well-being, Mill becomes the precursor of postmodern doctrines of liberty. Whereas his theory of free speech was the most influential and controversial aspect of *On Liberty* in modern times, his theory of individuality is likely to be his most influential idea for postmodern times. Mill's *On Liberty* sees **self-reflexiveness** as part of well-being. It is thus justified both by the Liberal Legitimacy Test – it harms nobody – and by utility – it creates new possibilities of human experience.

Mill and postmodern liberty
We must be free to interpret our own lives. Liberty is self-reflexive.

> **QUOTATION**
>
> **THE FOURTH PROVERB OF WELL-BEING**
>
> *the … customs of other people are evidence of what their experience has taught them*
>
> cross reference O: 65; P: 122; N: 86

Mill's Dictionary of Well-Being

○ '*Customs*': Mill defines 'custom' as a second-hand interpretation of experience. To the extent that I follow custom, I am living a borrowed life, or living life on borrowed meanings. Custom is the alternative to interpreting experience for myself. More positively, the customs of others could be a useful ingredient in my search for my own interpretation, if regarded from outside. So, that is what they made of their experience; how well does that fit with my understanding of my own life?

Qualifications

Mill recognizes that these customs may embody a 'correct' understanding of someone else's experience. In other words, he is not the kind of thinker who sees all customs and traditions as wrong. Mill is not a crude modernizer. He does not think that custom is wrong because it is old-fashioned, or that the new will automatically be better. His argument is that custom may have been right for someone else, from their perspective on their own experience, but it still has to be tested afresh in each new life. The old understanding may be correct but 'unsuitable' for me.

Implications

Mill does not object to custom in itself. His objection is to compulsory custom, or tradition with a moral edge. If a society imposes customs, then it is also requiring people to interpret their lives in certain ways. Why should each generation live according to the self-understanding of their ancestors? In other words, Mill's case is that rigid customs deprive humanity of the new meanings that would arise if people were left to think for themselves. A custom-based society contributes fewer meanings to the history of mankind than an open society.

For instance, in the past, certain groups experienced their sexuality in the form of temptation. Others may experience sexuality as self-expression. One community may experience as solidarity what I experience as monotony. Your distraction may be my opportunity. Your irrelevance may be my new world. In Mill's terms, neither side can turn round to the other and insist that it possesses the only true interpretation. There is no right answer. The question, within the limits of harm to others, is which interpretation is 'suitable' to me.

QUOTATION

THE FIFTH PROVERB OF WELL-BEING

He who does anything because it is the custom makes no choice.

cross reference O: 65; P: 122; N: 86

Mill's Dictionary of Well-Being

o '*Choice*': Choice has become one of the main concepts in contemporary political and moral debate. Here is another example of Mill's increasing relevance to the future. He offers sharp definitions of the terms we are struggling to focus on ourselves. For Mill, choice is a function of individuality. A true choice expresses my nature, and not my way of belonging with others.

o '*No choice*': Mill produces a theory of false or inauthentic choice. A custom-based society reduces, or eliminates, true choice. If people select on the basis of traditions, then they are not becoming individuals.

Implications

* *All choice is personal.*

* *More choice means greater individuality.*

These views are actually quite extreme by ordinary standards. How often do people really ignore the usual judgements or requirements? How commonly do we really choose without any reference to the norm? According to Mill, true choice is difficult.

Modern politicians and economists often talk about extending choice or about giving people wider choices. For Mill, many of these choices would be deceptive. He would not be happy to accept conventional views of 'consumer choice' for example, because most of the time consumers choose within a tightly defined set of norms – fashion, say, or status or the values imposed by advertising. By Mill's standards, contemporary lifestyle would be no better than traditional customs. In fact, lifestyle would simply be a kind of instantaneous and short-lived custom.

According to Mill, we cannot say a society is free if people choose what is customary. Equally, a society is unfree if people choose only what is recommended by the adverts, or what impresses the neighbours. One example would be deciding to have children. If people have children because that is what they are meant to do, then they are making, in Mill's terms, 'no choice'.

QUOTATION

THE SIXTH PROVERB OF WELL-BEING

desires and impulses are as much a part of a perfect human being, as beliefs and restraints

cross reference O: 66; P: 124; N: 87

Mill's Dictionary of Well-Being

- o '*Desires and impulses*': Here again, Mill seems to anticipate Freud and modern psychology. Repressing desire makes us less human, not more civilized. Having no spontaneous impulses makes us wooden, not self-possessed.

- o '*A perfect human being*': This is an ideal, though not a recipe. Mill does propose and defend certain ways of being human against other ways. He does not believe that we will ever achieve perfection, but he has an ideal standard by which he judges. By perfection, Mill means the fullest possible expression of human nature – the more human, the better, within the rule of no harm to others.

Implications

There is a dialectic of well-being. Mill is not arguing that all desire is good, that we must act on impulse all the time. On the contrary, he is saying that we need both desire and belief, both impulse and restraint. In this argument, belief refers to considered views and judgements, formed in discussion with others. Desire is the immediate expression of a personal will, an instinctive force or drive. True self-control is achieved through the relationship between desire and belief, impulse and restraint. A person who eliminates desire is not showing self-control at all: what does he or she have to control in the first place?

Mill adds that strong impulses are not dangerous in themselves. They only become a problem if they are not 'properly balanced'. Nobody without strong desires will ever develop true self-control. Why would they need to? Both self-control and desire are part of our experience of humanity.

Here we can see that Mill both is and is not a relativist. He is a relativist in the sense that he will not impose on others a model for how to be a good human, but he is not a relativist, in that he defends a certain approach to the good life, an approach based on this idea of 'a perfect human being' as the fullest possible expression of every side of our nature, within the limits of harm to others. The more we approach perfection, the greater will be the utility of our lives in the vista of human history.

QUOTATION

THE SEVENTH PROVERB OF WELL-BEING

There is no natural connection between strong impulses and a weak conscience.

cross reference O: 66; P: 124; N: 87

Mill's Dictionary of Well-Being

o '*Conscience*': Throughout *On Liberty*, Mill argues against moralistic attitudes to other people. Most people's morality is a device for judging others, for rationalizing their dislike of what is different or challenging or awkward. However, Mill has his own theory of true moral conscience, which he defines here as the force which counterbalances impulse. A genuine conscience is personal. Authentic conscience is as individual as desire. Both desire and restraint express my own vision of life, my own personal project, in postmodern terms.

o '*Strong*' and '*weak*': Strength is a quality of the whole person, a way of being. Mill argues that all the elements of being are likely to expand together, or shrink in unison. Repression is, therefore, never a way of making 'space' for growth. If you suppress one aspect of a person, you are lessening their whole scope for being. Likewise, weakness is a quality of the whole being of a person.

Mill thinks in terms of strong character and weak character, rather than strong and weak characteristics. In this respect, his approach resembles that of the German nineteenth-century philosopher, Nietzsche.

Implications

Mill is proposing a theory of well-being as conflict. If society attempts to regulate our desires from the outside, we will never experience this proper conflict, between *my* desire and *my* conscience. A society that represses desires will also destroy the possibility of conscience. In a world where nobody is allowed to experiment with impulse and desire, there will also be no experimentation with conscience and no new ethical life. New moral values grow alongside new desires. The moral inventors are likely to be those with rich inner lives, with fierce impulses. They will be the people who need to find a new balance.

More emotional does not mean less rational. People with stronger feelings will probably have richer reasons in response. Mill's theory of personality centres on wholeness of being.

Mill and modern psychology
Well-being means wholeness. The greater the wholeness, the greater the well-being. Our being grows through conflict.

Mill has been accused of having only a negative approach to liberty, but that accusation seems unfair in the context of his theory of well-being. Liberty is the condition most friendly to the widest possible well-being of humanity, and Mill has quite a full and rounded vision of that well-being. He is at least as concerned to create a new language for individuality as he is to deconstruct the claims of moralistic censorship and traditional authority. Mill is not merely anti-authoritarian; he has an affirmative ideal of the human individual.

Mill has also been accused of failing to connect his liberal theory with his utilitarian philosophy. Again, this seems unfair in the context of his arguments about individuality. He is a liberal because of his utilitarianism – in the sense that he sees liberty as the proper condition for the maximum promotion of the interests of humankind.

Applied liberty

In this chapter, we look at the way Mill draws his arguments together. In the later parts of *On Liberty*, he focuses on issues of his own day and on more specific recommendations and anti-recommendations. This more applied discussion runs from the end of Chapter III ('Of Individuality') through Chapter IV ('Of the Limits of the Authority of Society over the Individual') and Chapter V ('Applications'). Though the sections are lively and provocative, they do not change substantially the argument or introduce new concepts or terms.

Since Mill is now concerned with practical applications, it seems most appropriate to look at these parts in the context of specific cases from our own day. We can then ask whether the ideas still apply to particular cases. We have already seen that the general concepts are still very much alive; but perhaps the more applied side of *On Liberty* has dated.

THE 'FREEDOM TO BE YOURSELF' CAMPAIGN
On the BBC News for Wednesday, 10 January 2001, it was announced that:

> *A jury has unanimously cleared a veteran nudist*
> *campaigner of being a public nuisance.*

The man was Vincent Bethell, founder and leader of the Freedom to be Yourself Movement. To protest against the arbitrary requirement to be clothed in public, he had staged naked protests and had previously been found guilty by magistrates. This was his first jury trial and the ten men and two women had cleared him of the charge. In court, Bethell exclaimed: '*Being human is not a crime.*' He was warned by the judge not to count his legal chickens: '*I wouldn't go away too much with that idea. It is simply not a public nuisance in these circumstances.'*

Reporting the event next day, *The Guardian* newspaper informed its readers that the defendant was *'the first person to stand trial in an English court naked'*.

The case clearly enters one area explored by *On Liberty*. Is this an eccentric individual being prevented from expressing his chosen identity? Or is he in fact harming others? In court, the prosecution claimed that his behaviour was bound *'to harm the morals of the public or their comfort, or to obstruct the public in the enjoyment of their rights'*. The Freedom Movement insisted (*The Guardian*, 28 July 1999) that there was no harm to others in *'non-sexual peaceful public nudity'*. In one incident, where Bethell perched naked on a lamppost, a passer-by was quoted as saying: *'Onlookers were not shocked by the protest and the protesters were doing no harm.'*

There was a dark side to the story, as well as a lighter touch. Prior to the trial, Bethell had been kept in solitary in Brixton prison for two months because, as a remand prisoner, he refused to wear clothes:

> *He said by telephone that he was locked naked in his 11ft by 7ft cell most of the day and night ... He had no visitors, he said, being kept out of the visitors' centre for fear of offending inmates and visitors, and no outside exercise, for fear he cut his feet.*
>
> *The Guardian*, 9 November 2000

How does Mill's applied discussion relate to this case? In his chapter on applications Mill rather reluctantly adds a few remarks about decency, mainly pointing out that *On Liberty* is not concerned with the question of indecency but with the wider problem of individual self-expression. He does say that there are 'many acts' that are fine in private but not in public. His tone is restrained. He calls such indecency *'a violation of good manners'* (cross reference **O**: 109;

P: 168; **N**: 117). He then declares that as such it can be stopped. With an audible murmur of distaste or even embarrassment, Mill notes: '*Of this kind are offences against decency; on which it is unnecessary to dwell.*'

Mill would clearly not be a member of the Freedom to Be Yourself Movement. In fact, he might well see such a campaign as a dangerous travesty of liberal ideals. At the same time, if he did object to Bethell's actions, it would be under the low-key heading of 'violation of good manners', rather than in any terms like harm to public morals. Clearly, good manners belong to their time; they can change, and if so, then the limits of permissible action can change. It does seem unlikely you could justify keeping a person in solitary confinement for bad manners. So far we can see how Mill's language still offers a more refined and humane tone than that in which moral controversy is currently conducted.

Other passages might at least make us hesitate before applying legal sanctions to such campaigners. Mill laments that 'individuals are lost in the crowd'. He adds positively that:

QUOTATION

Precisely because the tyranny of opinion is such as to make eccentricity a reproach, it is desirable, in order to break through that tyranny, that people should be eccentric.

cross reference O: 74; P: 132; N: 93

Does wearing no clothes count as a desirable eccentricity? One suspects, from the squeamish passage on public decency, that for Mill it may not! But he does give us a different question to ask. Instead of simply wondering whether these displays do no real harm, we can also ask whether this is possibly an admirable eccentricity, in a time of conformity whether this is just a misguided person who has confused independence with rudeness. *On Liberty* does not really give ready answers to such cases. The aim of the book, carried through in its more applied later stages, is to make us ask richer questions and use more refined terms.

The case of the naked campaigner is a classic illustration of the fact that Mill's question, from his Chapter IV 'Of the Limits to the Authority of Society over the Individual', remains *our* question:

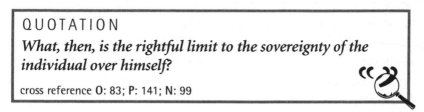

QUOTATION
What, then, is the rightful limit to the sovereignty of the individual over himself?

cross reference O: 83; P: 141; N: 99

Mill's arguments encourage us to keep asking this question and not to substitute our unthinking reactions for this process of inquiry. It may be that the Freedom to Be Yourself campaigner has violated good manners to the point where we are entitled to stop him. On the other hand, maybe we should express our distaste in ways that fall short of actually restraining him.

Mill is not in favour of a 'stiff upper lip' world where everyone ignores everybody else and pretends that nothing unusual is happening. We might find humane ways to voice our annoyance, if we decide that this person is not really harming anyone, but is still failing to meet appropriate standards:

QUOTATION
What I contend for is, that the inconveniences which are strictly unseparable from the unfavourable judgement of others, are the only ones to which a person should ever be subjected for that portion of his conduct and character which concerns his own good, but which does not affect the interest of others in their relations with him.

cross reference O: 86; P: 144; N: 101

Possibly, we should subject him to the 'inconvenience' of our disapproval. On the other hand, it could be that *we* should suffer his behaviour as a necessary 'inconvenience':

QUOTATION

But with regard to the merely contingent or, as it may be called, constructive injury which a person causes to society by conduct which neither violates any specific duty to the public, nor occasions perceptible hurt to any assignable individual except himself, the inconvenience is one which society can afford to bear, for the sake of the greater good of human freedom. If grown persons are to be punished for not taking proper care of themselves.

cross reference O: 91; P: 149; N: 105

You might well feel that wearing no clothes is 'not taking proper care' of oneself. In fact, the prison authorities seem to have used this as a pretext for denying Bethell exercise rights: he might cut his feet in the yard. Mill's passage encourages us to wonder if the yard should not have been made safer for him! It also makes one sense a certain bad faith in such reasons.

Mill makes us realize how serious a thing it is to limit 'the sovereignty of an individual'. Every time we feel we have to restrain someone like the Freedom to Be Yourself activist, we are deciding to lessen the sum of human freedom. It may be justifiable, if we really feel he is denying our access to a decent social environment, but we must always use the least possible intervention, and we must be honest about our motives. Are we sure it is his bad manners that are intolerable? Or are we just outraged by his non-conformity:

> QUOTATION
>
> *There are many who consider as an injury to themselves any conduct which they have a distaste for, and resent it as an outrage to their feelings.*
>
> cross reference O: 93; P: 151; N: 106

We may feel distaste, but is it really doing us any harm – or are we harming ourselves by the excessiveness of our own reactions and our inability to control our feelings of disgust? *On Liberty* retains an extraordinary power of refining and enriching the coarse terms in which we often express our reactions to other people's awkward behaviour.

BOUND TO STAY SILENT? MILL AND THE WHISTLEBLOWER

On Tuesday, 16 March 1999, Europe awoke to a startling announcement:

Europe was left decapitated last night as the entire European Commission resigned en masse after a devastating report by an independent commission.

The Guardian

The commission's President, Jacques Santer, came from an emotional commission meeting just after midnight.

BBC News

The news was bleakly grand. This was a world-scale event, the disappearance of the entire ruling body of one of the great blocs. The BBC was excitedly grim:

The European Union has been plunged into deep crisis following the resignation of all 20 Commissioners … it was still unclear how the EU would continue.

But all of this had begun with the actions of one minor European Union official, a Dutch accountant named Paul van Buitenen. In early December 1998 this official wrote an internal report specifying widespread fraud and mismanagement. Fearing that it would be suppressed, he passed a copy of this report to the Green Party in the European Parliament. In response, he was suspended on half pay. It was noted in reports that when officials had been accused of corruption, they were suspended on full pay.

The Greens circulated the report, and on 17 December 1998 the EU Parliament tabled motion of no confidence in the Commission. After initial delays and denials, the President, Jacques Santer, admitted irregularities may have occurred.

An inquiry was established. Meanwhile, van Buitenen had been accused of 'imparting information to unauthorised and non-competent persons'. The BBC reported on 6 January 1999 that:

> *The Commission says he was suspended for breaking his contract by releasing details of the inquiry.*

An EU spokeswoman explained in justification that: '*The report should have been kept secret while the case is under investigation.*' At the same time, the 'whistleblower', as he became known, faced other pressures. *The* Guardian noted (11 January 1999) '*barely veiled allegations that he is mad*'. He was said to be a religious fanatic and a political extremist:

> *I admit that part of my motivation is that I am a Christian ... I did not realise that was an offence. Then they say I am an extreme right-winger ... I am a member of the Green party.*
>
> The Guardian, 13 October 1999

Yet when the inquiry was reported, van Buitenen's claims were endorsed, with spectacular results.

Mill did, in fact, consider the argument about people binding themselves to limit their own freedom of action and expression. Should the whistleblower have honoured the 'gagging' clause in his own contract, and kept his report secret until it had been considered by the requisite authorities? His acceptance of the original job contract was, in Mill's terms, a 'mutual agreement' and:

QUOTATION

… it is fit, as a general rule, that those engagements should be kept. Yet, in the laws, probably, of every country, this general rule has some exceptions … engagements which violate the rights of third parties … injurious to themselves.

cross reference O: 113; P: 172; N: 121

In other words, contracts should generally be honoured, but there must be exceptions. People cannot be bound by agreements which deny them basic freedoms or which bind them to act against the real interests of others, or to harm themselves. The EU had argued that this dissident had been suspended for 'breaking his contract', but Mill specifically insists, in reply, that a person cannot always be held to '*the fulfilment of the contract*' (cross reference O: 115; P: 174; N: 122).

Freedom of expression, and of individuality, can sometimes override the literal 'fulfilment' of the terms of a contract. For example, following Mill, we could argue that the interests of the citizens of Europe would have been harmed if the information had *not* been revealed. We could also argue that van Buitenen's own interests required the disclosure: could he have withstood the counter-pressure on his own?

Several of Mill's arguments seem to come together around this famous case. The disclosure of the information is an example of free expression, which has turned out to serve the 'permanent interests' of the wider world. From the hostile responses of the authorities, it seems reasonable to wonder if they would ever have acted on this report had it not been made public. Their counter-action, through the media, seems to have involved the attempt to stigmatize individuality as well as to suppress freedom of discussion. It seems that expression and individuality still go together. Those authorities that try to prevent expression seem also to be antagonised by difference, or even eccentricity.

Does the story have a happy ending? The whistleblower was re-employed, but apparently not given back his original job:

> *He was reinstated by the commission … but was moved to an accounting unit dealing with the non-controversial ordering of furniture.*

> *The Guardian*, 13 October 1999

He wrote a book, which the authorities tried to prevent being published. Is this a further case of punishing individuality and restricting expression? The authority argued that there were good reasons, at least for suppressing the book:

> *The commission has no desire to suppress freedom of speech, but the civil rights of those who are the subject of allegations must be protected.*

Was van Buitenen's book prejudicing the fair trial or assessment of those accused of corruption? If so, the censorship might be justified on grounds of 'harm to others'. But is that the real motive? A court decided in favour of the whistleblower.

Mill recognizes cases where harm to others is not a good enough reason for censorship:

> QUOTATION
>
> *... it must by no means be supposed, because damage, or probability of damage, to the interests of others, can alone justify the interference of society, that therefore it always does justify such interference.*
>
> cross reference O: 104; P: 163; N: 114

Even if van Buitenen's book damaged the interests of some others, that might still not be a good enough reason to prevent its publication. This is surely a case of 'probability of damage' or even possibility of damage. But again that could be outweighed by the value to society of letting a neglected fragment of the truth be heard, even if it is expressed intemperately.

In his *Autobiography*, Mill warned that *On Liberty* was a book for the future. We remain citizens of Mill's future, and we still need his arguments.

REFERENCES AND FURTHER READING

Mill, John Stuart, *Autobiography* (Penguin, 1974).

Mill, John Stuart, *Utilitarianism* (including Bentham and Austin), edited and introduced by Mary Warnock (Collins, 1962).

Ackerman, Bruce, *Social Justice in the Liberal State* (Yale University Press, 1980).

Beck, Ulrich, *Risk Society* (Sage Publications, 1992).

Berlin, Isaiah, *Four Essays on Liberty* (Oxford University Press, 1969).

Britton, Karl, *John Stuart Mill* (Penguin, 1953).

Collini, Stefan, *The Public Moralists* (Oxford University Press, 1991).

Giddens, Anthony, *Modernity and Self-Identity* (Polity Press, 1991).

Gray, John, *Mill On Liberty: A Defence*, second edition (Routledge, 1986).

Gray, J. and Smith, G.W. (eds), *Mill: On Liberty In Focus* (Routledge, 1991).

MacIntyre, Alasdair, *After Virtue* (Duckworth, 1981).

Nozick, Robert, *Anarchy, State and Utopia* (Basic Books, 1974).

Rawls, John, *Political Liberalism* (Columbia University Press, 1993).

Riley, Jonathan, *Mill On Liberty* (Routledge, 1998).

Ryan, Alan, *John Stuart Mill* (Macmillan, 1987).

Skorupski, John (ed.), *The Cambridge Companion to Mill* (Cambridge University Press, 1998).

Ten, C.L., *Mill On Liberty* (Oxford University Press, 1980).

Thomas, William, *John Stuart Mill* (Oxford University Press, 1985).

Williams, Raymond, *Culture and Society* (Chatto & Windus, 1958).

Classic essays by R. H. Hutton, James Stephen and Isaiah Berlin are reprinted in Alan Ryan (ed.), *Mill* (Norton Critical Edition, 1997).

INDEX

BEGINNER'S GUIDES

DARWIN'S *ORIGIN OF SPECIES* – A BEGINNER'S GUIDE

GEORGE MYERSON

No single book has had more impact on the modern world than Darwin's *On The Origin of Species by Means of Natural Selection, or the Preservation of Favoured Races in the Struggle for Life*. From its publication in 1859, Darwin's great work has shaped the modern vision of man and nature. *The Origin of Species* defines and justifies Darwin's theory of evolution as the scientific alternative to the biblical view of creation.

George Myerson's lively text:

* Investigates the background to Darwin's *The Origin of the Species*
* Offers a clear and concise summary of the whole book
* Gives close-up explanations of the most important arguments
* Focuses for the reader the central concepts such as 'the struggle for existence', 'natural selection' and the evolution of 'instincts'.

This *Beginner's Guide* enables you to decide for yourself what you think about Darwin's *The Origin of Species* and its evolutionary vision of life on earth.

BEGINNER'S GUIDES

NIETZSCHE'S *THUS SPAKE ZARATHUSTRA* – A BEGINNER'S GUIDE

GEORGE MYERSON

Nietzsche's *Thus Spake Zarathustra* is the most controversial book in the history of philosophy. With its many famous lines and statements – including the notorious news that 'God is dead!' – *Thus Spake Zarathustra* has provoked and enthralled generations of readers. Literary masterpiece and angry polemic, manifesto and poem, personal confession and historic prophecy: what will you find in Nietzsche's visionary theory?

George Myerson's lively text:

* Investigates the background of *Thus Spake Zarathustra*
* Offers a clear and concise summary of the whole book
* Gives close-up explanations of the most important arguments
* Focuses for the reader the central concepts such as the superman, redemption and eternal return.

Other related titles

SMITH'S *WEALTH OF NATIONS* – A BEGINNER'S GUIDE

MARTIN COHEN

Few books have had more impact on the modern world than Smith's celebrated inquiry into the origin of the *Wealth of Nations*. Originally published in the year of the American Declaration of Independence, it rapidly became the most popular book of its time, marking the transition of political society from economic naïvety to financial sophistication.

Martin Cohen's accessible guide to the text:

* Offers a clear and complete summary of the main arguments presented by Smith

* Describes the social and cultural context of the work

* Explains the key concepts of modern economics